Edexcel A2
Religious Studies

BRUTON SCHOOL
FOR GIRLS

BORROWER	Date given out	Date Returned	Staff Initials

Sarah K. Tyler and Gordon Reid

Philip Allan Updates, part of the Hodder Education Group, an Hachette Livre UK company, Market Place, Deddington, Oxfordshire OX15 0SE

Orders
Bookpoint Ltd, 130 Milton Park, Abingdon, Oxfordshire, OX14 4SB
tel: 01235 827720
fax: 01235 400454
e-mail: uk.orders@bookpoint.co.uk
Lines are open 9.00 a.m.–5.00 p.m., Monday to Saturday, with a 24-hour message answering service. You can also order through the Philip Allan Updates website: www.philipallan.co.uk

© Philip Allan Updates 2007

ISBN 978-1-84489-442-0

First printed 2007
Impression number   5   4   3   2   1
Year   2012   2011   2010   2009   2008   2007

Cover illustration by John Spencer

Printed in Malta

Philip Allan Updates' policy is to use papers that are natural, renewable and recyclable products and made from wood grown in sustainable forests. The logging and manufacturing processes are expected to conform to the environmental regulations of the country of origin.

Contents

Introduction

■ ■ ■

Introduction

About this guide

This question and answer guide has been written as a resource aimed specifically at helping you in your revision of A2 Philosophy, Ethics and New Testament papers in religious studies for the Edexcel specification.

There are 24 questions, with A-grade responses. They are followed by examiner comments (preceded by the icon e), which will help you to identify the particular strengths and weaknesses of the answers. Remember that it is possible to achieve an A grade for an essay in several ways, but the same principles apply.

We have aimed to make these essays representative of the answer that a top-grade student at sixth-form level should be able to produce in an exam. You may feel that you want to add to them or include different material. However, all of them would gain full marks if written under timed conditions. Remember that you have only 35 minutes to write each essay in the exam, so there is not a lot to be gained by writing homework essays that are excessively long or include such high-level material you would not be able to remember it accurately in the exam.

It is a good idea for you to attempt to answer the questions yourself before looking at the answers and comments. In this way you can make a genuine comparison of your essays with those of other students working at different levels of achievement. As you work through the questions, read the answers and absorb the principles outlined in the examiner comments, and you will become increasingly familiar with the best approach to take. You will find that your own answers will improve with practice.

This book is ideally used in conjunction with the *Advanced Religious Studies* textbook. You will also find the religious studies Flashrevise and Topic CueCards helpful. These are all published by Philip Allan Updates.

The exam

The A2 exam is based on two units: Unit 3 Developments and Unit 4 Implications. The essays in this guide relate to Unit 3, which is a written exam of 1 hour 45 minutes. In the exam you have to answer three questions from a choice of 18, covering nine possible topics, of which you must choose at least two. The nine areas are Philosophy of Religion, Ethics, Buddhism, Christianity, Hinduism, Islam, Judaism, Sikhism and New Testament. Each topic covers two main areas and two questions will be set on each area. However, the questions will be either/or choices, so you cannot write more than one answer on a single subject area.

Assessment objectives

Edexcel sets out two assessment objectives — AO1 and AO2 — which allow the value of work to be judged.

AO1

AO1 is worth 60% of the marks. You earn these marks by showing that you know the subject, understand what is relevant to the question, can present evidence and examples, and can use technical language appropriately.

One of your aims during the course should be to identify and learn the facts and vocabulary you need to know. If you do this well, you will have mastered both the relevant knowledge and the terminology of the subject, and your AO1 material will be confident and convincing.

The demands of AO1 can be met only by solid learning, so students who have not absorbed the subject matter will be identified. Under exam conditions, you should be able to write 700 words to give yourself the best chance of fulfilling these criteria. Relating your answer directly to the question is vital in maximising your marks. Check the wording of the question to ensure that you are using the information in the right place and the right way, and not just repeating a block of memorised notes without reference to what you are being asked. Using examples appropriately can boost your marks, but too much narrative, use of ethical case studies or incidental anecdotes is not the best way to gain AO1 credit. Make sure the information you are presenting genuinely reveals you as an A-level candidate, so avoid chat and general knowledge.

AO1 asks you to show relevant *knowledge* of what you have been studying. For example, 'Explain how scholars have understood the term "religious experience".'

This question is asking you to demonstrate an understanding of terminology and the debates that lie behind the use of that terminology. A strong answer might consider whether a religious experience is a genuine occurrence or simply a strange feeling. Some philosophers have questioned the reliability of the testimony of those who claim to have had such an experience, while others suggest that, in the absence of convincing evidence to the contrary, we should believe what people say. You could raise issues such as the view that, if God really does exist, he would want to communicate with his people by religious experiences. Including the views of Aquinas, Hume, Hick, Swinburne, Dawkins and other scholars will add to the credit you will gain for demonstrating well-learned knowledge. It is important to show that you understand how and why the term is not easily defined, and that the range of different testimonies leads to problems about whether religious experiences can occur and what they reveal.

Look out for how new information fits into what you already know. Try not to leave a new set of facts or ideas without seeing how they relate to each other and what they add to your overall understanding of the subject. This means that you should review your notes and other materials regularly so you can incorporate your new information in the right place. Try to reorganise your file every week so that you always know if you are missing something and where material should go. Keep essays with the relevant topic rather than putting them in a separate file, as you should use them for revision.

AO2

AO2 is worth 40% of the marks. You earn these marks by sustaining a critical line of argument and justifying a point of view.

This is the more subtle part of the question and these marks are the ones needed to push you up to the higher-grade levels. Repetition of material from the AO1 part of the question cannot gain you further credit, so do not reduce AO2 to learning a list of criticisms that do not reveal your ability to assess strengths and weaknesses. Genuine evaluation grows out of an awareness of a range of views and an ability to assess which position is stronger. Save up something for this part of the question too, such as a scholarly quotation or an idea that you feel is decisive for the topic.

AO2 is the skill of *evaluation* and it is the more difficult skill to demonstrate. AO2 skills are built on AO1: you can evaluate only when you have sound knowledge and under-standing. AO2 breaks down into two: sustaining a critical line of argument and justifying a point of view. Each unit is based on key questions about that area of religion. None of these questions has ever been given an answer that satisfies all the experts in that area, which is why these questions are still studied. A critical line of argument aims to provide a possible answer to one of these key questions. The evidence is examined, other arguments are discussed, and reasons for and against the argument being proposed are given. This cannot be done in a sentence or two, which is why you are asked to sustain a critical line of argument.

When you are asked to evaluate, you are expected to have an opinion and to make a case for holding that opinion. This does not mean becoming a theologian or philosopher overnight. It is possible for an A2 student to come up with original thinking on a topic, but your point of view may be that those experts who propose one particular answer to a question are right and that those who do not are wrong. It is better to work on the assumption that evaluating a body of existing information is safer than making up your own evaluation, especially in the exam.

However, it is hoped that during your course you and your classmates will have contributed to the body of information you have absorbed. This will help you to remember it better than if you have never given it your stamp of individuality.

A typical AO2 question that would follow on from the AO1 question about the definition of the term 'religious experience' is 'Evaluate the view that religious experiences do not provide convincing proof of the existence of God'.

You need to recognise that you are not being asked to agree with or disagree with the claim — examiners do not care what you think personally, just how well you can weigh up the opposing responses to this claim. You must offer evidence that supports the claim and opposes it, before reaching a conclusion on which is the more convincing. For example, you might suggest that religious experiences do not occur today because there appear to be few, if any, cases of genuine experiences. Such experiences belonged to an age in which God was communicating in a different way with his people and they do not happen today because God uses sacred texts and religious leaders to reveal his word and will to his people.

Then give reasons that oppose the claim. For example, you could say that there are many occurrences of religious experiences worldwide, for which you may offer brief supporting evidence: the testimony of large numbers of people through the ages; corporate experiences of recent times, such as the Toronto Blessing; and the fact that such events have led many millions into faith in God. There is no reason to assume that God intended religious experiences to belong only to one age in history — there are several quotations from the Gospels to suggest otherwise.

Finally, you need to offer a reason why one view is stronger than the other, or, perhaps, to suggest that the view depends on how the speaker understands the term 'religious experience'. For example, if we take an anti-realist view of religious experiences, they are in the eye of the beholder — if the experient believes that he/she has experienced God, this is all that matters.

A key to meeting the AO2 objective is to learn what questions the experts are asking about the topic being studied and what some of the mainstream answers are. This should be clear from the teaching you receive and the reading you do. As soon as you notice that an opinion is being expressed, you should ask yourself what arguments and evidence are being put forward to support it.

You are not expected to arrive at a definitive answer, or to come up with something original, but you must show that you are aware that there is a case to be answered, whatever your personal views may be. It is acceptable to refer to your own opinion, but that must be in direct response to, or supported by, scholarly opinion.

Anything you can write which is relevant to the exam question and which meets the criteria for AO1 and AO2 will gain you marks. You will not lose marks for work that fails to do this — marking is not negative — but you may waste time and opportunities. For example, if you are writing about the Ontological Argument, biographical details about Anselm, however fascinating, are not going to gain credit. An understanding of his ontological proof is enough. Similarly, detailed narrative accounts of incidents in the life of Jesus will earn little credit unless you use them to illustrate key elements of his teaching.

Do not worry if you include AO2 material in the AO1 part of the question: it will still be credited. Examiners appreciate that high-level AO1 inevitably includes an evaluative element. However, if you provide AO1 material where AO2 is required, you are not meeting the demands of the question. Make sure that you practise applying AO2 skills to the material you have studied.

For the exam, your study should be aimed at giving you the confidence and the competence to meet these two assessment objectives, so you must ask your teacher if you are not sure how to do this.

Trigger words

Trigger words in questions enable you to identify the particular skills you have to use. They provide the instructions for how to answer the question. Some trigger words that may be used in questions are given in the table below.

	AS	A2
AO1	Describe	Analyse
	Examine	Clarify
	For what reasons	Comment critically
	Give an account of	Compare and contrast
	How	Define
	Identify	Differentiate
	Illustrate	Distinguish between
	In what ways	Examine
	Outline	Explain
	Select	
	What	
AO2	Comment on	Assess
	Consider	Consider critically
	How far	Criticise
	To what extent	Discuss
	Why	Evaluate
		Interpret
		Justify
		To what extent
		Why

Practise writing questions using these words and rewrite your teacher's questions using trigger words if they do not include them already.

You need to be aware of the difference between 'give an account of' and 'consider critically'. To give an account you draw essentially on your knowledge, which you may then be required to evaluate through 'considering critically'. Considering critically, assessing or commenting on involves drawing conclusions about the significance and value of what you have learned. There are certain phrases that you may find useful for this: 'This is important because', 'The most significant is...because', 'However...', 'On the other hand...', 'It is likely that...because', 'Therefore...', 'Nevertheless...', 'The implications of this are...'. As you work, keep asking yourself 'Why is this relevant to my answer?' and 'What are the implications of this view/issue?' Do not go onto automatic pilot, otherwise you will simply narrate facts or, worse, fiction.

Knowledge, understanding and skills

Trigger words help to focus your answer so that you can demonstrate that you have fulfilled the following overall aims of A2 religious studies.

Acquire knowledge and understanding of:
- the key concepts within the chosen area(s) of study and how these are expressed in texts, writings and/or practices
- the contribution of significant people, traditions or movements to the area(s) studied
- religious language and terminology
- major issues and questions arising from the chosen area(s) of study
- the relationship between the area(s) of study and other specified aspects of human experience

Develop the following skills:
- recall, select and deploy specified knowledge
- identify, investigate and analyse questions and issues arising from the course of study
- use appropriate language and terminology in context
- interpret and evaluate relevant concepts, issues, ideas, the relevance of arguments and the views of scholars
- communicate, using reasoned argument substantiated by evidence
- make connections between area(s) of study chosen and other aspects of human experience

Achieving a top grade

Examiners look for a number of key qualities that you need to show in order to achieve a high grade. Essays are marked according to the level descriptors listed below. Note that these descriptors will change for the 2010 exam. Your teacher will be able to download the new versions from the Edexcel website nearer the time. From 2010, A2 papers will be marked out of 50 (rather than 40), so the descriptors will take this into account.

AO1
- **Level 4** (19–24 marks): a full response to the task including a good range of relevant evidence presented within a clear and concise structure, with examples appropriately

deployed to highlight the main points, leading to a comprehensive and coherent answer; expressed accurately and fluently, using a range of technical vocabulary.

- **Level 3** (13–18 marks): a range of relevant evidence which is clearly structured, supported by well-chosen examples with sufficient breadth and depth to indicate broad understanding of the main issue; expressed clearly and accurately, using some technical terms.
- **Level 2** (7–12 marks): a sufficient range of evidence to show understanding of some key ideas or concepts, supported by examples, but limited in terms of the scope of the question; communicated with a sufficient degree of accuracy to make the meaning clear.
- **Level 1** (1–6 marks): some relevant knowledge that is deployed to show a basic understanding of the issue raised by the question, but limited in scope and imprecisely expressed.

AO2

- **Level 4** (13–16 marks): a coherent and comprehensive response in which scholarly opinion is carefully balanced by critical analysis, and where the argument is set (where appropriate) in the context of wider issues about religion; expressed accurately, fluently and using a range of technical vocabulary.
- **Level 3** (9–12 marks): a structured argument, justifying a point of view by reference to some analysis of other opinions, and showing a clear awareness of the issues raised; expressed clearly and accurately using some technical terms.
- **Level 2** (5–8 marks): arguments at a simple level to justify opinions, typically by reference to the views of others; expressed clearly and communicated with a sufficient degree of accuracy to make the meaning clear.
- **Level 1** (1–4 marks): an awareness of some relevant views in support of an argument, but given at a mainly descriptive level; imprecisely expressed.

Planning your essay

Your essay should be planned once the appropriate range of sources dealing with the topic have been read thoroughly, understood and compared. Homework essays are different from the essays you will be required to write in the exam, but they should not be so different that they are of no use to you for revision. Your teacher may want you to write long essays during the course so that your awareness of the topic can be widely tested. Remember that in the exam you will have only 35 minutes to write an essay, so make sure you write several timed essays during the course and attempt at least two timed practice papers.

When you do a timed essay, be selective about what you include from your source notes. Follow the pattern of the exam questions, whether they are single-section questions or are structured. However many sections there are, the marks are awarded as follows:

- **AO1**: 24 marks for knowledge and understanding. From your source notes, select the key features of whatever area of the specification is under consideration, keeping closely to the language of the question. Show that you know how various parts of the topic under discussion relate to each other.

- **AO2**: 16 marks for evaluation. Identify the range of arguments for and against the opinion or claim in the question, then clarify which you think is the most convincing or which position is easier to defend. What are the main arguments against the point of view you favour and why are you rejecting them? What is the alternative point of view, and why does it not present an overall convincing case?

If you give AO2 material in your answer to an AO1 question, it will still be credited, but as part of your overall AO1 marks. However, if you do this too much, you might use up your best evaluative points too early and be forced to repeat them for the AO2 part. Since material can only be credited once, this is a waste of time and marks. If a question asks for both AO1 and AO2 material, you can either shape the AO1 material around the AO2 material in each paragraph or keep them separate. The first option is more difficult but, if done properly, shows a good grasp of the subject.

Learning, revision and exam technique

As you prepare for your A2 exams, there are stages that your teacher will directly help you with and stages that you must be prepared to work on alone. In the end, teachers cannot go into the exam and do it for you. While they can give you information and guide you in the best practice for utilising that information in the exam, you have to make sure you have learned the material and developed an effective examination technique.

Lessons

It is initially your teacher's responsibility to select the right information for your needs, but you must take responsibility for the way you receive it and what you do with it after the class is over. This means that you need to develop good classroom habits. Ask questions about the material — this can help you to clarify what you have just heard, as well as clearing up misunderstandings. Ask questions about the implications of the material the teacher is covering and about how it relates to other aspects of the specification. Your classes also give you the opportunity to practise the vital skill of evaluation. You will hear many views expressed that might be different from your own. You can — in an empathetic (non-confrontational) way — evaluate them: 'Am I right in thinking that you believe X to be right because of Y?' Be prepared in turn for your views to be evaluated by others, and to explain why you hold them: 'I think that Z is wrong because if you take Y into consideration, the conclusion cannot be X.'

Homework tasks

Because you have to write in the examination — indeed, the written word is the only method for assessment — you must use homework tasks as an essential tool for refining your written skills. One of the most useful things you should be doing for homework is practising past questions, as they will enable you to become completely familiar with the way your board and specification require you to use the knowledge and under-standing you have gained. Your teacher can explain to you how he/she has marked your work in accordance with the principles laid down by the exam board and so you can gain some insight into the way the system works. Every homework exercise is an opportunity to learn the topic you are working on, so do not just stick it in the back of your file when it has been marked.

Independent learning and consolidation

Even the best teachers are not going to cover absolutely everything in the class time available, although they will use that time to provide you with almost everything you need to do well in the exam. However, it is the time you put in outside the classroom that is truly decisive. You may read an article that no one else in your class has seen, watch a television programme or just go over your class notes one more time and, in doing so, finally understand a difficult area. There is no doubt that the top grades usually go to candidates who are prepared to do something extra, rather than simply attending class and doing the work set.

Revision for the exam

It is never too early to start to revision. From the moment the first topic has been completed in class you should be making concise revision notes, learning quotations and making essay plans. If you leave it until the exams are looming, you will only have time to get the information into your short-term memory. You will feel far less able to deal with the unexpected, or to spend time in the exam ensuring that your written style is the best you can offer on the day. Revision techniques do, and indeed should, vary. Everybody learns and remembers differently, so do not be led into thinking that you should be doing it exactly the same way as everybody else. Experiment with a range of strategies but make sure they are multisensory, i.e. they involve using more than one sense. If you *read* through your notes, you are using one sense only. However, if you also rewrite them, read them out loud by working with another student or record them to listen to, then you are employing more than one sense. This will help to reinforce the work of the other senses, and your learning is therefore cumulative.

As you prepare for the exam, make sure that you are absolutely certain about key issues such as the day and time of the exam. You may think this is silly, but I have marked an exam paper on which a candidate wrote: 'Sorry about this, but I only just found out my exam was today.' This is not just a failure on the part of the school (if indeed she had not been told) but also a failure on the candidate's part not to make sure she knew the right day and time. Knowing dates well in advance enables you to make a revision plan, allocating specific tasks to each day as the exam approaches, so that your revision is never random or unplanned.

You also must be sure of what you will be required to do in the exam and how much time you have in which to do it. This is why you must practise exam questions under timed conditions. The best candidate may achieve a disappointing result because he/she did not work to time, writing one or two long answers, but resorting to a plan, notes or a 1-side-long offering for the others. If you have 1 hour 45 minutes to answer three questions, that means 35 minutes per question. Stick to this rule in all your timed work.

The exam

Remember that it is not over until you have written your last word, so do not be fatalistic about the exam. Keep calm and even if the questions are not the ones you hoped would come up, you can still use the material you have learned to write relevant answers to the questions that are there. Do what you are asked and nothing else. Do not panic and leave early, but *think*. Read what you have written and check it over for careless mistakes and misspellings. Ignore what everyone else is doing, even if they leave the room, faint or cry, and do not spend time in pointless postmortems after the exam. What's done is done at that stage, and you need to have peace of mind to prepare for your next paper.

Remember

- If you follow the instructions, are conscientious, thorough and communicate with your teacher, you should do well.
- People are there to help you. You need never feel alone in your quest for a good A-level grade. Every single member of staff at your school is on the same side as you, even if it does not always feel like it. There are also other ways of getting help. Look out for revision courses and 1-day or residential conferences, and ask if your teacher attends exam board meetings. Everyone wants you to do well.

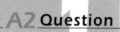

The Ontological Argument

Explain the key features of the Ontological Argument.
Evaluate the view that the strengths of this argument overcome
its weaknesses.   (40 marks)

The Ontological Argument is an a priori argument that reaches by logical steps a conclusion that is self-evidently true or logically necessary. It is deductive in form because the conclusion necessarily follows from the premises. The argument is also analytic — the truth (or falsity) of an analytic statement is completely determined by the meanings of the words and symbols used to express it. The Ontological Argument reaches conclusions about the existence of God that are based on the definition of God used in the premises. The most famous supporter was Anselm, who defined God as 'a being than which none greater can be thought'.

Anselm's argument was that a being that possessed all perfections must possess the perfection of existence. His argument runs like this:

P1: God is the greatest possible being *or* that than which nothing greater can be conceived.

P2: If God exists in the mind alone (*in intellectu*), a greater being could exist both in the mind and in reality (*in re*).

P3: This being would then be greater than God.

P4: Thus, God cannot exist only as an idea in the mind.

Conclusion: Therefore, God exists both in the mind (as an idea) and in reality.

Therefore, God must be a necessary being, meaning that he cannot not exist. It would be a logical contradiction to claim that God does not exist, since any being that has the property of necessary existence could not fail to exist.

Descartes saw the Ontological Argument in terms of necessary existence: just as man could conceive of his own existence, he could also conceive of the existence of a perfect being:

(1) I exist.

(2) In my mind I have the concept of a perfect being.

(3) As an imperfect being, I could not have conjured up the concept of a perfect being.

(4) The concept of a perfect being must therefore have originated from the perfect being itself.

(5) A perfect being must exist in order to be perfect.

(6) Therefore, a perfect being exists.

Kant argued that we must establish the existence of something before we can say what it is like, not the other way around. So if there is a perfect being, he must exist: 'Whatever, therefore, and however much our concept of an object may contain, we must go outside it if we are to ascribe existence to the object.' However, Descartes maintained that existence was predicated of God in the way that three angles are predicated of a triangle. To speak of a triangle without its angles is contradictory in the way that it is contradictory to speak of God without existence. Hence, Descartes developed Anselm's form of the argument, focusing less on the notion of existence *in re* and *in intellectu* and more on the notion that existence is a predicate of a perfect being.

In the twentieth century, Alvin Plantinga suggested that there may be an infinite number of possible worlds in which things are quite different. If God's existence is necessary, then he must exist in all these worlds. This is because God is *maximally great* and *maximally excellent* and cannot be conceived as being anything other than supremely perfect.

Supporters of the Ontological Argument speak of its three main strengths, which are centred around the notion that the argument can appeal to all sides. First, it holds out the hope of a proof. It is a deductive argument and is therefore valid for both believer and atheists.

Second, the definition of God as 'that than which nothing greater can be conceived' can be accepted by atheists and believers. As Anselm famously commented: 'Can it be that there is no such being, since the fool hath said in his heart "There is no God"...But when this same fool hears what I am saying — "A being than which none greater can be thought" — he understands what he hears...even if he does not understand that it exists.'

Third, supporters such as Normal Malcolm maintain that the argument reveals the impossibility of speaking of God as possessing anything other than necessary existence, since he cannot exist contingently or not at all. It is impossible to think of God as lacking any perfection — he must exist since he possesses all perfections.

However, in the eyes of many scholars, the Ontological Argument has fundamental weaknesses that outweigh its strengths. Critics have argued that the idea of God as 'that than which nothing greater can be conceived' is incoherent and inconsistent — in the face of significant problems such as the problem of evil, or apparently unanswered prayer. Arguably, the terms are meaningless anyway, because we have no direct experience of these attributes. Furthermore, the notion of God as that than which nothing greater can be conceived may be reasonable to a classical theist, but to some thinkers who have re-evaluated the idea of God, it is outdated. For example, process theology redefines God as 'the fellow sufferer who understands', which is a long way from the classical definition asserted by Anselm.

Moreover, the Ontological Argument is not a valid deductive argument. Definitions only tell us what God would be like if he existed. Definitions cannot establish whether he does in fact exist. When we say that existence is part of God's definition, we are merely saying that no non-existing being can be God. Replacing the word 'God' with 'the greatest island', Gaunilo argued that you can have true premises that lead to false conclusions. Thus:

(1) I can conceive of an island than which no greater island can be thought.

(2) Such an island must possess all perfections.

(3) Existence is a perfection.

(4) Therefore, the island exists.

David Hume dismissed the argument because it makes a false assumption about existence. He said that all existence was contingent and, therefore, limited. All things that could be said to exist could also be said not to exist. Existence was, therefore, a matter of fact, rather than analytical deduction.

In a similar way, Plantinga's view of God as a being of maximal greatness can be countered by the point that if there is a world of maximal greatness and a being of maximal excellence, there is no reason why there should not also be a being of maximal evil occupying all possible worlds.

The Ontological Argument is successful if we accept that the statements made are subjectively true statements, which operate as a language game in a particular form of life. So, for supporters of the argument, the claim that God is, *de dicto*, necessarily existent, is true within their particular 'form of life', as are other claims made within the religious system to which a believer subscribes. However, 'God necessarily exists' is a claim that may be rejected by critics of the argument as meaningless, unverifiable and unfalsifiable.

In my view, the weaknesses of the Ontological Argument outweigh the strengths. It succeeds only as an expression of what religious believers already hold to be true rather than offer proof to all that there is an objective reality that has the qualities to make it what we would term 'God'.

🄔 This answer highlights the importance of clear and comprehensive knowledge and understanding of the difficult issues and arguments surrounding this controversial notion. Initially, the candidate displays good understanding of the argument and incorporates the views of a range of scholars. He/she correctly outlines scholarly viewpoints without spending too long describing them in unnecessary detail. The style is fluent and makes excellent use of religious language. The candidate then offers a comprehensive examination of the evidence. Useful quotations support philosophical debate to produce a range of arguments and counter-arguments. The whole essay is well structured and fluently written, and the conclusion draws the threads neatly together.

🄔 **Do not feel that you have to mention every scholar and observation connected with this argument. If your essay is based entirely on Anselm's proof, it can be just as worthy of an A grade as this one, which ranges more widely. Although you can show greater knowledge by taking a broader view, you must avoid making your answer too long.**

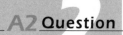
The Ontological Argument and argument from religious experience

'An analysis of arguments for the existence of God will result in valid philosophical reasons to believe in God.' Discuss and evaluate this claim with reference to both the argument from religious experience and the Ontological Argument.   (40 marks)

For an argument to provide conclusive philosophical reasons for believing anything, it must appeal to reason or to experience. We have conclusive philosophical reasons for believing that grass is green, because experience, guided by the physical senses, provides empirical evidence that this is so. Of course, the exception is when the grass is dry and brown, and experience and observation tell us that in this case it is not green. Reason and logic tell us that a circle is round, since roundness is the essence of circularity, and it is therefore logically necessary that it be so. The rules of mathematics similarly lead to conclusive philosophical reasons for believing that 2 + 2 = 4. Although some thinkers may argue that none of these examples needs necessarily be the case, it is more likely that most would agree that the philosophical reasons for believing them are generally sound, and accepted as such even by the most sceptical thinker.

Can we provide conclusive evidence for the existence of God in the same way? If arguments for his existence are subject to the same principles of reason, empirical proof or mathematics, then we should be able to do so. However, whether they are is clearly open to debate. The nature of the evidence may be considered to be flawed; the premises of the argument may only make the conclusion probable, not logically necessary; and the proponents of the argument may not be considered sufficiently objective.

The argument from religious experience is an a posteriori one. This means that it is based on experience, and if that experience is reliable, it may lead to reliable conclusions. However, if the experience is open to interpretation, not everyone may reach the same conclusions. The nature of religious experience is highly subjective and so it may, on first viewing, not be considered to be reliable. Since God is metaphysical, it may even be thought that talking about God is meaningless, let alone experiencing him. However, even if we argue that it is meaningful to talk of experiencing God, the debate is not over. Experience of the divine is inevitably subjective, since there are no agreed empirical tests that can confirm whether the best explanation for an apparently religious experience is God rather than anything else.

Philosophers may suggest many valid reasons for arguing that experience of God is essentially unverifiable and therefore cannot provide valid philosophical grounds for believing in his existence. First, the reliability of the experients needs to be taken into account. If they have a history of hysteria or delusion or have strong reasons to seek to justify their religious beliefs, we need to assess whether the reliability of their testimony might have been affected. Furthermore, religious experience may be the result of learned behaviour — copying others who appear to have had such an experience — or even wish-fulfilment, as Freud explained all religious feelings. Therefore, it is possible to argue that while religious experience, if verified, could be the most successful means for proving the existence of God, it is essentially flawed. Only the experients can say with any assurance that the experience they enjoyed originated in the divine rather than anything else, and even then they may be unduly, or even unconsciously, influenced by factors that lead them simply to infer the divine.

However, Richard Swinburne argues that unless we have good reasons to think that someone is not telling the truth, we should work on the principle that what he/she says is the case (these are his 'principles of testimony and credulity'). Just because we may not have shared a similar experience, or just because such experiences are unusual, is not sufficient grounds for doubting his/her testimony.

The Ontological Argument is an a priori argument that is based on reason rather than on experience, and is therefore deductive. Such an argument is philosophically valid if it is logically impossible to deny its conclusion, which is based on true premises. It depends therefore on an analytically true definition of God, which Anselm proposed as being 'that than which nothing greater can be conceived'. His argument can be formulated as follows:

P1: God is that than which nothing greater can be conceived.

P2: That than which nothing greater can be conceived contains all perfections.

P3: Existence is a perfection.

Conclusion: God exists.

According to Anselm's reasoning, the existence of God is analytically true, and therefore not simply a matter of faith. He rejoices that even if he were not able to believe in God by faith, he would have to acknowledge that his existence is logically necessary. However, Gaunilo accused Anselm of attempting to define God into existence simply by saying that God is supremely perfect, and a supremely perfect God must therefore exist. By the same logic, Gaunilo argued, *reductio ad absurdum*, that you could postulate that there is an island that is supremely perfect and therefore it must exist. Anselm also worked on the assumption that the definition of God was without doubt and that it included existence. While Descartes maintained that existence was necessary to God as three angles are to a triangle, Kant objected that 'existence' could not serve as a predicate (a defining characteristic that can be possessed or lacked). Therefore, Kant did not consider that the Ontological Argument could provide valid philosophical reasons to believe in God, since it worked on a false premise — that existence is to God what circularity is to a circle, or a valley to a mountain.

The two arguments offer completely different approaches to proving God's existence and each works if the grounds on which they are based are not flawed. For those who have a religious experience, the existence of God is proved beyond doubt if there is no better explanation for the experience. For others, there may seem to be more likely explanations, drawn from more regular experience. The Ontological Argument would be foolproof if its premises were analytically true, but even believers may be hard-pressed to accept that God's existence is necessary *de dicto* — simply by definition. Aquinas argued that we must know of God's existence before we can say anything about his attributes, while, according to Anselm's reasoning, God's existence is one of his attributes, which remains a matter of debate.

This impressive response demonstrates that the candidate understands the demands of the question and has tailored some well-learned information to suit his/her needs. The key to this essay is ensuring that you address the question specifically. Many candidates see the words 'religious experience' and 'Ontological Argument' and provide the examiner with the sum of human knowledge on the two arguments without any indication that they have read the question. This candidate appreciates that the question concerns the nature of proof.

Be prepared to combine more than one argument for the existence of God, but make sure that you have learned enough about each argument for the more traditional questions that focus on one argument only.

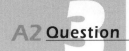

Religious experience (1)

Analyse the main concepts of religious experience as an argument for the existence of God. To what extent does this argument provide convincing proof of the existence of God?   (40 marks)

Religious experiences are beyond ordinary empirical explanation and usually take place within a context of religious expectancy and hope. Religious experiences may be individual and subjective, where a person becomes aware of a transcendent reality, or corporate, where a gathering of people experience powers beyond normal under-standing. Religious experiences produce feelings that defy expression: they are ineffable. St Teresa of Avila described her experiences: 'God establishes himself in the interior of this soul in such a way that, when I return to myself, it is wholly impossible for me to doubt that I have been in God and God in me.'

Scholars have always been puzzled by religious experiences. Schleiermacher said they offer a sense of the ultimate, an awareness of wholeness, a consciousness of infinite-ness and finiteness, and a feeling of absolute dependence. William James said that religious experiences inspire a range of emotions — happiness, fear and wonder — towards God. The person has feelings of great joy and a desire to belong to God. John Wesley wrote of his experience: 'I felt my heart strangely warmed. I felt I did trust in Christ, Christ alone, for salvation; and an assurance was given me, that He had taken away my sins, even mine.'

Paul Tillich said that a religious experience was a feeling of 'ultimate concern', a feeling that demanded a decisive decision from the person receiving it. Rudolf Otto used the word 'numinous' to describe religious experience — something holy or 'wholly other' than the physical world. In the Bible, the most famous example of a religious experience is Saul's conversion on the road to Damascus: '...suddenly a light from heaven flashed around him. He fell to the ground and heard a voice say to him, "Saul, Saul, why do you persecute me?"' (Acts 9:3–4).

As an argument for the existence of God, religious experience is naturally a posteriori. It is based on the premise that to experience something is in some way evidence of the reality of that which is being experienced. This seems reasonable from the perspective of our experience of the world and of everyday things, and we operate on the basis that our experience can be trusted. If it is the case that experience of things in the empirical world is an indication of the reality of those things, proponents of the argument from religious experience claim that the same can be applied to experience of God. The premises of the argument can be set out as follows:

P1: Experience of X indicates the reality of X.

P2: Experience of God indicates the reality of God.

P3: It is possible to experience God.

Conclusion: God exists.

The overwhelming testimony over the centuries to accounts of religious experiences contributes significantly to the power that such an argument may have. If God has made himself known to millions of people, then there are conceivably good reasons to believe that God exists. In order to challenge this argument it is necessary to demonstrate that all these accounts are unreliable or false.

The form of the argument outlined above is inductive and those who believe that religious experiences are proof of the existence of God usually argue *inductively*. This means that they look at the subjective testimonies of individuals who claim to have had religious experiences in order to find similar characteristics and then infer that they can be explained only in terms of the existence of God. Thus, Richard Swinburne argues inductively that it is reasonable to believe that God is loving and personal and would seek to reveal himself to humanity as an act of love and to enable people to bring about good: 'An omnipotent and perfectly good creator will seek to interact with his creatures and, in particular, with human persons capable of knowing him.'

Swinburne suggests that religious experiences can be felt empirically, through our senses, and interpreted non-empirically, through our 'religious sense'. Thus, if we are told that someone has had a religious experience, we should believe that experience has taken place, even if someone else has had a different experience or none at all. Brian Davies observes: 'We certainly do make mistakes about reality because we fail to interpret our experience correctly; but if we do not work on the assumption that what seems to be so is sometimes so, then it is hard to see how we can establish anything at all.'

Although those who support religious experience as proof of the existence of God claim that, if God manifests himself in a direct way, then he must exist, the real problems are why God should reveal himself, if indeed he does, and why we should believe people's accounts of religious experiences.

In terms of believing people's testimonies about religious experiences, Swinburne offers the 'principle of credulity' — unless we have overwhelming evidence to the contrary, we should believe that things are as they seem to be. He argues also for the 'principle of testimony', namely that we should, unless we have real cause to doubt otherwise, believe what people say: 'In the absence of special considerations the experiences of others are (probably) as they report them.'

Swinburne identifies three types of evidence that give grounds for saying that a person's testimony is unreliable — for instance, if the circumstances surrounding the experience are unreliable (e.g. hallucinatory drugs) or that we have particular evidence to suggest that the person is lying. Finally, it may be that the experience could be explained in terms other than God, for instance, the person was suffering from a fever. He argues that most religious experiences do not take place in these circumstances and that we should believe the testimony of those who have had a religious experience. Thus, religious experiences do provide a convincing proof for the existence of God.

On the other hand, religious experiences cannot be tested objectively. We cannot carry out a scientific experiment to determine whether they have, in fact, revealed God. They are therefore ambiguous and can be interpreted in various ways. Wittgenstein used the notion of 'seeing-as', suggesting that each person sees their experiences differently. Some may think that they have experienced God; others may think that they have experienced something else. This makes all such testimonies about religious experience potentially unreliable because we can mistake what we experience.

There are further strong arguments against the validity of religious experience as proof of the existence of God. First, if God does not exist, there can be no experience of him. Moreover, it is impossible to know if people are experiencing God since there are no tests to verify their claims. Finally, religious experiences may be the manifestation of psychological needs. Richard Dawkins argues: 'If we are gullible, we don't recognize hallucinations or lucid dreaming for what it is and we claim to have seen or heard a ghost; or an angel; or God...such visions and manifestations are certainly not good grounds for believing that ghosts or angels, [or] gods are actually there.'

Religious experiences provide a strong, but ultimately unconvincing, proof of the existence of God because we cannot test the validity of the testimonies objectively or empirically. Yet for those who have had a life-changing religious experience, it is utterly convincing proof. Swinburne is more certain: 'I suggest that the overwhelming testimony of so many millions of people to occasional experiences of God must, in the absence of counter-evidence, be taken as tipping the balance of evidence decisively in favour of the existence of God.'

ⓔ This kind of question requires thorough preparation as it is easy to muddle the two parts, but this candidate successfully avoids any confusion. The first part is a comprehensive analysis of the notion of religious experience as proof of the existence of God, which clarifies the argument and offers a range of views. The candidate identifies clearly the most important features and expresses them accurately and fluently. In the second part, he/she offers a lucid and concise evaluation of the argument with critical analysis through a range of alternative scholarly viewpoints and balanced reason, using a wide range of religious and philosophical terms. The conclusion is well structured and draws the arguments together clearly.

ⓔ **Note that this question focuses on religious experience as an argument for the existence of God, not just on types or descriptions of religious experience. Recognising this fact can make the difference between gaining a top A grade and a low B grade.**

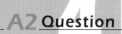

Religious experience (2)

'Religious experiences are meaningless because they can never
be proved to have happened.' Discuss and evaluate this claim.   (40 marks)

'The argument from personal experience is the one that is the most convincing to those
who claim to have had one. But it is the least convincing to anyone else, especially
anyone knowledgeable about psychology' (Richard Dawkins).

The argument from religious experience is an a posteriori one that is based on
experience. Schleiermacher defined religious experience as one that yields a sense of the
ultimate, and Rudolf Otto coined the term 'numinous' to cover descriptions of specific
religious experiences that offer evidence on the 'wholly other' nature of God. William
James observed that religious experience draws on the common store of emotions —
happiness, fear and wonder — but is directed at something divine. However, the nature
of religious experience is highly subjective, although some scholars such as Brian Davies
have suggested that this need not be a stumbling block: 'Just as I can reasonably say
that there is a bed in my room because I have encountered it, so I can reasonably
say that there is a God because I have directly encountered him.'

Those who argue that testimonies of religious experiences are meaningless base their
views on the fact that these experiences are not subject to empirical testing and are not,
therefore, factually verifiable assertions. This was a view supported by Flew, who argued
that religious believers are stubborn in their beliefs, although statements concerning
religious experiences have no objective meaningful content. For others, the testimony
of religious believers is especially biased and questionable and cannot be counted as
reliable or meaningful evidence. In *The End of Faith*, Sam Harris writes: 'We have names
for people who have many beliefs for which there is no rational justification. When their
beliefs are extremely common we call them "religious", otherwise they are likely to be
called "mad", "psychotic" or "delusional".'

Richard Dawkins goes further, claiming that testimonies of religious experiences are
simply the manifestation of mental or psychological needs. Religion may be an illusion
created by the human brain to enable us to cope with fear of death and the unknown:
'If you've had such an experience, you may find yourself firmly believing that it was real.
But don't expect the rest of us to take your word for it, especially if we have the slightest
familiarity with the brain and its powerful workings.'

Writing in *Language, Truth and Logic* in 1936, A. J. Ayer dismissed claims to religious
experience on the grounds that although people having religious experiences 'is
interesting from the psychological point of view, it does not in any way imply that there
is such a thing as religious knowledge'. Ayer's position was that if someone claims to

have seen God, he/she tends to do so as though it were the same as claiming to have seen a yellow patch. However, while 'the sentence "There exists here a yellow-coloured material thing" expresses a genuine synthetic proposition which could be empirically verified, the sentence "There exists a transcendent god" has...no literal significance'. Ayer criticised the approach of the religious experient which moved from asserting that he/she was experiencing a particular religious emotion to the assertion that there existed a transcendent being who was the object of that emotion.

However, supporters of religious experiences claim that there are ways in which the experiences can be seen as meaningful. For instance, using A. J. Ayer's notion of a weakened verification principle, it could be argued that a religious experience can be meaningful because it is, in principle, verifiable. This may be manifest by John Hick's principle of eschatological verification or Keith Ward's claim that God may, one day, verify the religious experiences himself. Alternatively, religious experiences may fall within the scope of Wittgenstein's notion of 'seeing as', or could come within the notion of a 'blik' — an unverifiable and unfalsifiable way of looking at the world, which represents, according to Hick, 'ways of regarding the world which are in principle neither verifiable nor falsifiable'.

Others, such as Richard Swinburne, argue that it is perfectly meaningful for God to make himself known to people, in order to bring about the good, and to intervene personally in the lives of individuals out of his love for them: 'An omnipotent and perfectly good creator will seek to interact with his creatures and, in particular, with human persons capable of knowing him.'

In his principles of testimony and credulity, Swinburne suggests that testimonies of religious experiences are meaningful because, unless there is overwhelming evidence to the contrary, we should believe that what people say is true. There are no grounds for claiming that the testimony of religious believers is any less reliable than that of non-believers. Moreover, should we be surprised that religious experiences are more likely to be experienced by religious believers? After all, they know what to look for and are more likely to recognise the experience when it happens. Indeed, if we wait until we have a common interpretation of every experience, we will end up doubting all our experiences. Brian Davies observes: '...if we do not work on the assumption that what seems to be so is sometimes so, then it is hard to see how we can establish anything at all.'

In a similar vein, although it may be difficult to verify a testimony of a religious experience, it is equally difficult to falsify it and prove it did not occur. If it is possible to have any kind of experience of God, then it must be reasonable to assume that some experiences of God actually are experiences of him. Swinburne observes that '...our experience ought to tip the balance in favour of God'.

It may be possible to test the meaningfulness of a religious experience by examining the effects that it had on the life of the person who experienced it — for example, the life-changing experience of Paul after he saw a vision of Jesus: 'As he neared Damascus on his journey, suddenly a light from heaven flashed around him' (Acts 9:3). However, it may be that many claims of religious experiences are just attempts to satisfy deep psychological, emotional and physical needs and are meaningless because, as Sam Harris suggests: '...while religious people are not generally mad, their core beliefs absolutely are.'

However, it does not follow that all testimonies of religious experiences are meaningless because, as Swinburne observes, God '...will love each of us as individual creatures, and so has reason to intervene...simply to show himself to individuals, and to tell them things individual to themselves'.

The answer starts well, with a thought-provoking and controversial quotation, and the candidate displays confident understanding of the arguments, highlighting the views of several scholars and using supporting quotations. He/she clarifies the issues and technical terms without spending too long describing them in unnecessary detail. The pace of the essay is good and the candidate moves smoothly from one view to the next with fluency and excellent use of religious language. He/she correctly emphasises the distinction between notions of truth and falsehood and gives a balanced view of both sides of the argument, supported by external evidence and scholarly opinion. The carefully chosen quotations support philosophical debate to produce a range of arguments and counter-arguments. The essay is well structured and fluently written and the conclusion draws the two sides neatly together.

This complex question links two distinct areas of study: religious experience and religious language. The answer requires comprehensive knowledge and understanding of all the main issues involved in ascertaining the meaning and accuracy of statements and truth-claims concerning religious experiences.

Life after death (1)

> Compare and contrast the immortality of the soul and the resurrection of the body. To what extent is one of these a more convincing position than the other?
>
> (40 marks)

The immortality of the soul is the view that a human being has two aspects: a mortal, physical body and an immortal, spiritual soul, which is the real person and contains all the important factors that make a person a unique individual. (For the purposes of this work, the soul is also closely identified with the concept of the mind and the terms are used together.) In *Phaedo*, Plato suggested that the body belongs to the physical world and, like all physical matter, it will one day turn to dust. However, the soul belongs to a higher realm where 'eternal truths', justice, love and goodness last forever. In a similar way, Maritain said: 'A spiritual soul cannot be corrupted, since it possesses no physical matter...the human soul cannot die.'

For Kant, the purpose of existence was to achieve the 'summum bonum' or complete good, and this could not be achieved in the space of one short lifetime. Kant suggested that God is under a moral obligation to grant humans eternal life in order to enable humanity to achieve this good. He said: 'The summum bonum is only possible on the presupposition of the immortality of the soul.'

This position is known as dualism — the notion that a person's personal identity or soul is distinct from his/her body. However, many theologians disagree and suggest that personal identity is strongly linked to the physical body. Aquinas observed: 'The natural condition of the human soul is to be united to the body.' The resurrection of the body is the view that eternal life depends on an act of God's divine love. Resurrection is nothing to do with resuscitating corpses. It is the re-creation by God of the person, not as a physical being but as a spiritual being. The resurrected Christ appeared before his disciples with a body, he talked and ate with them, they touched him and they saw his scars. Yet he was different: he could appear and disappear, and he was beyond death: 'Look at my hands and my feet...touch me and see; a ghost does not have flesh and bones, as you see I have' (Luke 24:39). Later, Paul said that the resurrected body was spiritual and would last forever: 'For the trumpet will sound, the dead will be raised imperishable, and we shall be changed. For the perishable must clothe itself with the imperishable, and the mortal with immortality' (1 Corinthians 15:52–53).

Neither position is more convincing since both views ultimately depend on what is meant by being human. Human beings have a physical body and a mental or spiritual mind/soul. The physical body can be seen and identified but the mind/ soul cannot be analysed in the same way. The problem is whether mind and body are of one and the same nature (monistic) or have two natures (dualistic).

Dualists claim that humans have composite natures — part of them is material (physical body) and part is non-material (mind/soul). Descartes said that the body is spatial but not conscious, whereas the mind is non-spatial and conscious, with feelings and thoughts. He believed that body and soul were separate but that the state of the body affected the mind/soul and vice versa.

This presents a dilemma: if humans have two natures, do they both end on death or does one or both survive? Materialists, such as Gilbert Ryle, reject the notion that body and mind are separate entities. Ryle spoke of the soul as being the 'ghost in the machine' and advocated 'philosophical behaviourism' — that is, all mental events are really physical events interpreted in a mental way. Thus, the 'mind/soul' is not a separate entity but just a term meaning 'what we do with our physical bodies'.

The heart of the problem lies in the matter of what constitutes personal identity and what constitutes a person. Obviously, on the level of observation, the body is the means by which we can identify a person. If this is the case, then the philosophical problem arises that if people are to have eternal life in the meaningful sense of being 'them', then they will require both a body and a mind/soul. In such a case, the immortality of the soul alone is insufficient for bodily and personal continuity and must be rejected.

On the other hand, are people to be limited in their identity to the body? If the body is resurrected, is it the same person? Is there bodily continuity or is the resurrected body just a spiritual copy of that person? If it is a copy, then continuity is lost. Moreover, what about the appearance of the body? Will the resurrected person be the same in every way or are some things changed? For instance, can the blind see, are the old made young, are all diseases, handicaps and defects cured? If so, is this still the original person? If not, then bodily continuity is lost and the resurrection of the body must be rejected.

However, perhaps the question is a moot one, since unless we are convinced that the notion of life after death is convincing at all, we cannot get as far as considering whether a resurrected body or an immortal soul is the most reasonable way of understanding it. Unsurprisingly, A. J. Ayer observed that the notion of a soul — an imperceptible part of humans that apparently lives on after death — is a meaningless idea, but once we begin to consider the idea of life after death, it is questionable whether even the phrase itself is meaningful. In *New Essays in Philosophical Theology*, Anthony Flew observed that to speak of life after death implies that there had been no death at all. After all, we do not speak of dead survivors — to survive is to live and to die is to fail to survive. Furthermore, the function that belief in an afterlife may serve for the individual may also cast a shadow on its meaningfulness. If it is a belief that comforts and reassures believers in the face of the uncertainties of death, then it does not matter which form they believe it may take.

In the light of such considerations, it is not particularly useful to ask which form of the afterlife is more convincing, but rather whether the prospect of an afterlife is convincing at all.

e This type of question requires thorough preparation because it is easy to confuse its different demands. This candidate offers a comprehensive comparison of the notions of immortality of the soul and bodily resurrection, highlighting the views of Aquinas and Kant, ably supported by useful quotations and textual evidence. This is amplified and expanded by the precise references made to the views of other scholars in order to clarify the arguments. The candidate clearly identifies the most important features and expresses them accurately and fluently. He/she explores the main strengths and weaknesses, offering critical analysis through a range of alternative scholarly viewpoints and balanced reason, using a wide range of technical vocabulary. The conclusion binds the answer together and demonstrates clearly that the student understands the wider implications of the question.

e **Make sure that you address the key point of the question — which position is more convincing? This involves reviewing strengths and weaknesses as well as considering the wider picture.**

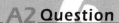

Life after death (2)

'Life after death is a meaningless concept.' Examine and comment critically on the accuracy of this statement.

(40 marks)

Anthony Flew, in _New Essays in Philosophical Theology_ (1955), questioned whether it is meaningful to talk about life after death. In his view, if there is life after death, then, in a sense, there is no death at all, since death and life are two mutually exclusive categories — you cannot 'survive death'. So can we speak meaningfully about life after death?

Life after death is certainly an important aspect of human existence. We find it hard to accept that this life is all that there is and there seems, within us, to be a need for more, a time to fulfil our potential. We place high value on human life, and it is hard to conceive of it ending. As John Hick observed: 'If the human potential is to be fulfilled in the lives of individuals, these lives must be prolonged far beyond the limits of our present bodily existence.'

It is not just religious believers who are concerned with life after death. Many who would not consider themselves to be religious find the prospect of a postmortem (after-death) experience highly desirable. Why? Certainly the thought of death has a powerful, and sometimes frightening, effect on us. Not only do we find it hard to accept that this life is all that there is, but we feel that there ought to be something beyond this life that gives meaning to our earthly existence. We value life highly in a moral and ethical way, talking about the sanctity and quality of life and about the need for the moral law to be balanced, with good rewarded and evil punished, if not in this life, then in the next. Indeed, many religions make the afterlife a central aspect of faith. For instance, in Christianity, the afterlife is a gift from God: 'Following as a corollary from faith in a good and loving God…that which has been begun by God during man's life on earth, the creation of sons fit for full fellowship with him, will be continued and completed by God, in his own time and in his own ways, beyond the confines of earthly life' (Robert McAfee Brown).

Since it is impossible for someone to prove that there is life after death, the problem remains one of verification. Can we ever talk meaningfully about something that we cannot empirically prove to be true? Some would say we can and would point to the testimonies of people who claim to have had a near-death experience, or have remembered past lives or contacted the deceased through mediums and psychic experiences. However, none of these testimonies has been verified scientifically and they remain on the fringes of mainstream thought.

John Hick suggested that life after death can, however, be discussed meaningfully in terms of what he called 'eschatological versification'. In this view, although we cannot verify the truth or otherwise of life after death at the present time, when the end comes, then we, potentially, will be able to verify it. Thus, in Christianity, for example, the Bible teaches that the dead will be raised again and live forever in a new world: 'And I saw the dead, great and small, standing before the throne...and the Holy City, the new Jerusalem, coming down out of heaven from God' (Rev. 20:12ff).

But can we talk meaningfully about the dead being raised back to life? Hick thought so in his 'replica theory', in which he claimed that life after death, in the form of a replicated body, may be logically conceivable — not in this physical world but in a resurrection world. He believed that if someone dies and appears in a new world with the same memories and physical features, it is meaningful to call this replica the same person, for an all-powerful God would be able to create a perfect replica of a person, with all their thoughts, memories and characteristics, living in a world of resurrected people. In *Philosophy of Religion*, Hick wrote that God can re-create someone '...as a resurrection replica in a different world altogether, a resurrection world inhabited only by resurrected persons'.

The key to the problem of the meaningfulness of the concept of life after death ultimately depends on what we mean by life and death. Hick's theory suggests that such existence depends on a re-joining of the body and the soul by an act of God. This was, in effect, what Aquinas suggested centuries earlier: 'Since, therefore, the natural condition of the soul is to be united to the body...it has a natural desire for union with the body, hence the will cannot be perfectly at rest until the soul is again joined to a body. When this takes place, man rises from the dead.'

However, others have argued that the body and soul are separate. Plato argued that we have an immortal, pre-existent soul, which encountered true reality before becoming imprisoned in the physical body. At birth, the soul forgets its previous life, but through a process known as 'anamnesis' ('non-forgetting') it can be reminded of the nature of true reality. The soul is immortal and immutable, unlike the body, which is a physical entity that changes and is imperfect. Death is the final separation of body and soul, when the soul can re-enter the eternal realm of truth from which it came. 'Our soul is of a nature entirely independent of the body, and consequently...it is not bound to die with it. And since we cannot see any other causes that destroy the soul, we are naturally led to conclude that it is immortal' (Descartes).

For the empiricist, even to speak of a soul is a meaningless exercise, since no observations can be made to verify its existence. A. J. Ayer claimed 'that [to say] there is something imperceptible inside a man, which is his soul or his real self, and that it goes on living after he is dead' is therefore meaningless (*Language, Truth and Logic*, 1936). Other scholars have highlighted the incomprehensibility of such talk, arguing that the very phrase 'life after death' entails an impossible contradiction, since life and death are two mutually exclusive states. As in a plane crash there are those who die and those who survive, there are no 'dead survivors', a logical impossibility that is tantamount to what life after death involves.

However, there is another possibility that life after death can be referred to meaningfully. This is known as the 'coherence theory of truth'. In this view, the meaningfulness or otherwise of a statement concerning life after death does not depend on its verifiability in the physical world. Instead, its truth or falsity is related to the other statements with which it is associated. For instance, to speak of a 'soul' and to try to see it as an object in the physical world would be to misunderstand the nature and meaning of the word. We can speak meaningfully of life after death as part of a religious language game, which gives the concept meaning to those who participate in the game. In this way, life after death can be spoken of meaningfully, especially if it refers to the quality of life that is available to those who share a set of beliefs. As Richard Swinburne observes: '...there are plenty of examples of statements which some people judge to be factual which are not apparently confirmable or disconfirmable through observation'.

[e] This question highlights the need for comprehensive knowledge and understanding of the issues surrounding the differing viewpoints. It looks at two areas of study: life after death and religious language. The candidate makes a solid start and shows that he/she understands the arguments by presenting the views of several scholars and using religious terminology fluently. He/she is right to emphasise the distinction between notions of truth and falsehood and does not spend too long describing them in unnecessary detail. The candidate mentions the wider implications of the argument and makes a balanced and reasoned evaluation based on a range of ideas and scholarly debates. The conclusion is balanced and encourages the reader to appreciate the complexity of the arguments.

[e] **You cannot answer this question properly without some knowledge of religious language. You need to have considered carefully the implications of 'meaningful' and 'meaningless' in the specific context of the afterlife. This will allow you to show skills beyond those of many other candidates.**

Religious language (1)

'Religious language is meaningless.' Analyse and evaluate this
claim, with reference to the verification and falsification debates.   (40 marks)

Religious language is language which is used to describe God and the nature of religious
belief. Yet it comes from our common, everyday language and raises the question that,
if God is above and beyond all human experience, how can our ordinary words speak
sensibly about the supreme deity? We have no special words for God, so we must find
ways of making our language work effectively when talking about God. Inevitably, the
question arises of whether we can ever talk meaningfully about God?

Religious language can be 'cognitive', making factual assertions that can be proved true
or false, including statements that believers say contain meaningful, factual content such
as 'God exists' or 'God loves us'. Alternatively, religious language may be 'non-cognitive',
that is, statements that can be interpreted in another way, such as symbols, metaphors
and ethical commands. They are not as factually true but can be understood by
individuals and the community to which they belong. The truth or falsity of such
language depends on the context, for instance 'Obey God to be sure of heaven' or 'Jesus
is the Lamb of God'.

The biggest question facing religious language surrounds the issue of meaninglessness.
Critics have argued that religious language is meaningless because it does not deal with
factually verifiable assertions. Supporters say that it is meaningful because it is not
always supposed to be understood cognitively and it can be verified, at least as far as
believers are concerned.

Wittgenstein's picture theory of language (a statement is meaningful if it can be defined,
or pictured, in the real world) inspired the Vienna Circle in the 1920s. These philosophers were known as the logical positivists, who offered an understanding of language
that they called the verification principle. By this, they meant that statements were to
be considered meaningful only if they fulfil one of three criteria. First, the statements
can be true by definition, such as 'A circle is round'. Second, the statements can be true
mathematically . Third, they can be synthetic statements that can be verified by testing
— for instance, empirical statements that can be proved true by the senses (e.g. 'fire is
hot') — or they can be analytically true, that is, provable by deduction, such as 'There
are mountains on the far side of the moon'.

Thus, for the logical positivists, a statement is deemed meaningful only if it can be
verified by observation or experience. All other statements cannot be verified and are,
therefore, meaningless. And herein lies the problem. Religious statements about God
are neither analytically true, nor can they be verified by observation, so, for the logical

positivists, religious language is meaningless. There are no observations that can verify a statement such as 'Jesus is the only way to the Father' since it is a belief claim, which is not dependent on empirical evidence. Although for the believer it is highly significant, this is not the same as being able to say that it has factual value.

However, the verification principle is itself problematic. For instance, it cannot absolutely verify all scientific laws or historical statements. Indeed, there is no way to verify whether the verification principle itself is true. Even its great champion, A. J. Ayer, was forced to propose a weakened form of the verification principle that allows something to be deemed meaningful if it is, in principle, verifiable. The verification principle therefore lost credibility, as Brian McGee observed in *Confessions of a Philosopher*: 'People began to realise that this glittering new scalpel was, in one operation after another, killing the patient.'

Ayer's compromise did allow religious language to achieve more credibility. Keith Ward was able to argue that God's existence could be verified in principle since God himself could verify it. Similarly, John Hick argued that eschatological verification would confirm religious truth in the afterlife. Moreover, many religious language claims are historical and if other historical statements were verifiable in principle, then statements such as 'Jesus died on the cross' or 'Muhammad is the final prophet of Allah' would also have to be accepted as meaningful.

The failure of the verification principle led to a new development: the falsification principle. It was proposed by Anthony Flew, who argued that instead of showing that a statement is verifiable, the onus should be on the speaker to say what would, in principle, count in making it false. He famously observed: 'What would have to occur or to have occurred to constitute for you a disproof of the love of, or the existence of, God?' Flew used the parable of the gardener to illustrate how religious believers were responsible for not facing up to evidence that may prove their claims to be false, and instead accused them of hiding behind statements such as: 'The ways of God are incomprehensible.' Flew argued that believers must be able to say what would cause them to question their claims about God: 'Now it often seems to people who are not religious as if there was no conceivable event...the occurrence of which would be admitted by sophisticated religious people to be a sufficient reason for conceding..."God does not really love us then".'

Flew maintained that a statement about God that could be made to fit into any circumstances, such as 'God moves in mysterious ways' has no meaningful content. In *Faith and Knowledge,* Hick wrote: 'In order to say something which may possibly be true, we must say something which may possibly be false.' Flew thought that the stubbornness of religious believers to have their assertions challenged would mean that religious language would always be meaningless. However, critics have argued otherwise. R. M. Hare suggested that religious statements are 'bliks': ways of seeing the world that are true for the believer. Hick commented that bliks are useful because they represent 'ways of regarding the world which are in principle neither verifiable nor falsifiable — but modes of cognition to which the terms "veridical" or "illusory" properly apply'.

Basil Mitchell, in support of religious language, argued that many believers do recognise and accept challenges to faith. The believer accepts the need to be open to serious conflict and challenge, but, in faith, will keep to what he/she believes to be true in his/her heart. Thus, when the believer asserts, 'I know that my claim that God loves me is reasonably challenged from every side, but my personal encouter with God enables me to hold to the truth of that claim', that religious language becomes truly meaningful.

e In order to answer this question you need comprehensive knowledge and under-standing of the issues involved in ascertaining the meaning and accuracy of religious-language statements and truth-claims. The candidate shows clear under-standing of the arguments, giving the views of several scholars and using religious terminology fluently. He/she makes a confident start and clarifies the issues and technical terms, outlining scholarly viewpoints in sufficient detail. The pace of the essay is good and the candidate moves smoothly from one view to the next with fluency and excellent use of religious language. He/she is right to emphasise the distinction between notions of truth and falsehood, and the various arguments are clearly laid out and supported by external evidence and scholarly views. The philo-sophical debate is underpinned by quotations that offer a range of arguments and counter-arguments. The whole essay is well structured and fluent.

e **You should aim for a balance between verification and falsification and make sure that you evaluate both positions.**

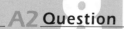

Religious language (2)

Discuss critically the contribution of symbol and myth to the problem of religious language.

(40 marks)

Cognitive language makes factual assertions that can be proved true or false, for example, 'God exists'; 'God loves us'; 'God will execute a final judgement'. When believers make such claims, they presumably intend to make assertions that they at least consider to be objectively true. Anthony Flew observed that they are not 'crypto-commands, expressions of wishes, disguised ejaculations, concealed ethics, or anything else but assertions'. Non-cognitive language, on the other hand, makes assertions that are to be interpreted in some other way, as non-literal modes of expression. It is language that serves some other function than expressing factually, objectively true claims. Symbol and myth are two such ways of using language. It is a matter of debate whether religious language is intended to be cognitive or non-cognitive, but if it does deal with matters that are beyond objective, scientific testing, then it must include a non-cognitive dimension. If it is entirely cognitive, believers will run into problems when they attempt to verify their claims in a literal way.

A symbol can be described as a pattern or object that points to an invisible metaphysical reality and participates in it (Erika Dinkler-von Schubert). Symbols therefore identify — point to the concept they are conveying — and participate — share in some way in the meaning of that concept. Symbols may be pictorial, abstract, verbal or active (a symbolic action). So, for example, the cross (a central symbol in the Christian tradition) immediately identifies for believers the death of Jesus, but it does more than simply point to it in a factual way. It participates in it by bringing to the believer's consciousness what Jesus's death signifies, for example salvation from sin, atonement and God's love for the world.

Paul Tillich used the example of a national flag as a symbol that conveys nationalism, patriotism and national identity. It is more than a sign that simply provides information or instructions, such as a traffic light or street sign. In the same way, religious symbols express what the believer feels about what that symbol conveys. Signs are to do with facts; symbols transcend facts and should therefore not be interpreted literally, which leads only to misunderstanding.

Symbols are therefore subtle modes of communication that belong to higher levels of communication and, while they do not belong exclusively to religious language, they are of particular value to discourse that deals with issues that are beyond the factual and objective, giving them meaning rather than dismissing them as meaningless.

However, although symbols are useful ways to communicate truths that go beyond the factual world, their interpretation can pose difficulties. Symbols can become the focus of worship in themselves and the object of veneration — for example, when a believer maintains that it is baptism that conveys salvation, rather than representing salvation that has already been gained. Symbols may be trivialised and their original meaning lost and they can become outdated, like myths. With this in mind, Paul Tillich wrote: 'It is necessary to rediscover the questions to which the Christian symbols are the answers in a way which is understandable to our time.'

Myths embody and express claims that cannot be expressed in any other way, frequently making use of symbol, metaphor and imagery in a narrative context. They are not to be thought of as conveying information that is 'not true', but rather as a means of conveying concepts that go beyond basic true–false descriptors to express that which is otherworldly. Mythological language was also used by the biblical writers to speak of eschatological events as well as to describe events that took place before history — the creation, the flood and the tower of Babel are primary examples.

Myths, however, are often criticised as being outdated, and in the 1920s Rudolf Bultmann famously claimed: 'It is impossible to use electric light and the wireless and to avail ourselves of modern medical and surgical discoveries and at the same time, to believe in the New Testament world of demons and spirits.' He argued that it was necessary to access the kerygma, or the core of religious truth which is concealed by myth, and to do this religious language must be demythologised. He claimed that myth made it harder for the twentieth-century mind to grasp the truth of the biblical message. However, mythological language is so deeply engrained in religious language that it may be impossible to dispense with it altogether, and it is more important to consider how it should be interpreted than to be concerned about trying to establish what 'really happened'.

Mythological language poses even more difficulties for the contemporary thinker than symbol does, often serving as a focus of conflict between believer and non-believer. However, this need be the case only when the conflict is between whether the mythology should be taken literally. The tensions that are commonly exposed today tend to highlight the differences between fundamentalist or evangelical Christians and atheists, and are at the extreme end of the debate. It is easy to see one as right and one as wrong, rather than as different, but not necessarily wrong, ways of looking at the world.

Perhaps the use of language games may solve the problems of myth and symbol (non-cognitive language in general). For the believer, myth and symbol are the best ways to speak about religious belief, whereas the empiricist has no need of this kind of language. But as with all language games, the key is knowing the rules. For empiricists, mythological language will be nonsense if they try to interpret it using empiricist tools, just as for the believer, there are times when the literal language of the empiricist fails to communicate spiritual truths about God and his relationship with the world.

The candidate makes clear use of scholarship and relevant examples, blending positive and negative evaluation of symbol and myth effectively in order to reach a considered conclusion. He/she demonstrates immediately a solid understanding of the fundamental principles of religious language before going on to a discussion of myth and symbol specifically. Thorough learning of the relevant material means that the candidate does not have to rely on generic or vague claims about religious language.

Remember that you may not be offered a choice of religious-language topics. As with this question, examiners can target two specific issues, so do not limit your revision if you plan to answer questions on religious language.

Atheism and agnosticism

Distinguish between agnosticism and atheism. Analyse a critique of religious belief and consider critically whether it better supports an agnostic or atheistic view.

(40 marks)

Atheism means literally 'without/no God'. There are many reasons why people may hold an atheistic position. Some may hold alternative spiritual views that do not allow room for the God of classical theism, while others may feel that religious belief is irrational or can be explained in terms of other phenomena or social structures. Atheists may never have held a belief in God, or they may have had what seem to them to be good reasons to abandon their belief, possibly because they have suffered experiences that posed serious challenges to their faith. Whatever their reasons for maintaining that there is no God and that religious faith and practice are therefore empty of any real significance, the atheist has decided that there is apparently no room for doubting the non-existence of God.

It has recently become popular to distinguish between an atheist and an antitheist. While atheists may personally reject belief in God but hold that it has meaning for other people, antitheists argue that because belief in God is delusional or dangerous, it is not enough simply to reject it for themselves. As Richard Dawkins commented: 'I just want people to stop believing.'

The term 'agnosticism' was coined in the nineteenth century by Thomas Huxley. An agnostic may claim to be open to the possibility of knowledge leading to belief rather than non-belief, but may not be able to say what it would take for him/her to make that move. Hence, it is possible to say that agnosticism is merely another form of atheism, since an agnostic has made no decision in favour of belief in God. However, for those who consider agnosticism to be a legitimate intellectual position, this would not be acceptable. An agnostic may maintain that he/she could choose to believe if sufficient evidence were presented, although what would constitute sufficient evidence may not be clear.

Durkheim's functionalist sociological theory of religion argues that religion plays a function in society: to unite and preserve the community. He defined religion as: 'A unified system of beliefs and practices relative to sacred things...beliefs and practices which unite into one single moral community called a church, all who adhere to them.' He likened a religious community to a primitive clan that worships a totem which symbolises God and the unity of the clan. The clan and God are one and the same. Hence there is no separate entity called God, and thus God does not exist. What does exist is a unified social system that believes it owes its being to God. This belief is expressed in shared rituals, values and identity, and it discourages change.

Another sociological explanation of religion, which consequently denies the existence of God, was offered by Marx, who argued that God is an invention of the human mind in order to satisfy emotional needs. Only by loving one another rather than God can man regain his humanity and reclaim the powers that belong to man but which man has ascribed to God. According to Marx, religion is used by the ruling classes to dominate and oppress their subjects, offering them an illusion of escape. Marx maintained that only when a revolution overthrows the ruling class, and religion is abolished, can the oppressed masses be liberated, and recognise their need to rid themselves of religious belief, which is nothing more than 'the opium of the masses'.

Any atheistic argument, or critique of religious belief, appears to work on the assumption that while belief in God cannot be conclusively verified, non-belief in God and alternative explanations for religious belief are subject to verification. However, both atheist, and theist, use the same data and are concerned with the question of the existence of a metaphysical entity. If a metaphysical entity cannot be conclusively verified, surely it cannot be conclusively falsified either, and in principle the atheist's position is no more intellectually sound than that of the theist. A sociological argument attempts to explain religious belief in terms of society and thus deny the existence of an objectively real deity, but in so doing, Marx and Durkheim simply offer an alternative explanation rather than a conclusive disproof of the existence of God.

In this respect, their arguments must be more supportive of agnosticism than atheism. While it is possible that religious phenomena and the existence of God may be explained in terms of society's functions, such an explanation fails to explain all the features of belief in God. Religious believers distinguish between membership of their religious community and belief in God; their loyalty is to God, not to the community. Yet Durkheim suggests that loyalty to the community is man's primary commitment. His theory cannot therefore explain how religious believers are sometimes prepared to go against society and even to reject it in order to remain faithful to God. Furthermore, society changes constantly, whereas beliefs about the nature of God are timeless and unchanging. Religious believers are often prepared to stand by ideals that appear anachronistic to non-believers, and yet to believers they are an essential part of their belief in God.

Therefore, sociological critiques may offer a possible explanation for certain religious phenomena. They cannot serve as conclusive atheistic arguments, but rather they support an agnostic perspective that still has room for belief in God, even if the function of religion itself is considered questionable. However, for an antitheist such as Richard Dawkins, an agnostic position is almost as untenable as a theistic position, since from his perspective nothing about the existence of God can be verified, and nothing about the role of religion in society can be deemed to be helpful or valuable. From Dawkins's perspective, therefore, all critiques of religious belief should point firmly to a denial of the existence of God as well as the failure of all religious systems to do anything but encourage 'extremism, violence and terror'.

e The candidate demonstrates wide knowledge and understanding and meets both demands made by the question. He/she deals confidently with the terminology and the content of the sociological critiques of religion. The evaluation is well sustained and the candidate clearly recognises the philosophical demands made upon religious belief by the atheist and agnostic. Inclusion of up-to-date material on the popularist work of Richard Dawkins is valid and enhances the more traditional atheistic material.

e **Make sure that you distinguish between an argument for the non-existence of God and a critique of religious belief. It is perfectly reasonable to argue that religion serves a social or psychological function, but this does not lead to the conclusion that God does not exist. On the other hand, critiques of religious belief are rarely compatible with traditional classical theistic belief.**

Religion and morality

Examine and critically assess two critiques of the link between religion and morality.

(40 marks)

The association between religion and morality is complex, but it is nevertheless, to a considerable extent, taken for granted. However, there are many aspects to the relationship that philosophers and theologians have identified as problematic. For example, we might consider whether is it possible to be religious but not moral, or moral but not religious. What is the relationship between God and goodness, and would the existence of a moral law presuppose the existence of a supreme moral lawgiver? Perhaps, most significantly, how far does the moral teaching of religions accurately reflect what may be thought to be the moral will and intentions of God?

All these questions are important for assessing whether the link between religion and morality is positive. Many have asserted that it is not, and we can trace this back to Plato's Euthyphro Dilemma, which poses a serious challenge to classical theistic views of morality. The dilemma asks: 'Does God command X (where X is a moral command) because it is good, or is X good because God commands it?' Both positions highlight problems for the relationship between God and morality.

In the case of the first position, goodness exists as something separate from God and to which God needs access in order to make a moral command. God is the means by which humans receive moral knowledge, but that knowledge does not come directly from God's morally good nature. That knowledge, although communicated by God, comes from outside his nature — he is not wholly good, although he may conform to that standard of goodness he receives and passes to humans. Clearly in this case, God is not the guarantor of moral goodness and in some way his nature is qualified. He cannot bring goodness into being apart from the goodness that he accesses from outside himself. Therefore, this is surely not the traditional God of theism.

In the second position, there is no doubt that God is the direct source of moral knowledge. God's commands establish what is good, and nothing can be good unless God commands it. The answer to the question 'What is good?' has to be 'What God commands'. However, if this is the case, then the answer to the question 'Why is God good?' has to be 'Because he obeys his own commands', which seems to be a limited understanding of God's goodness, since saying 'God is good' is essentially the same as saying 'God does what he commands'. We still have not learned much about God, since he could effectively command anything he liked and it would, by virtue of his command, be good, and he would be good if he obeyed it.

The second position assumes that a moral action is one that is willed by God; he is the source of morality and humans act morally when they fulfil God's will obediently. This view effectively argues that a moral law is made right by virtue of divine command. The God who makes the command is an omnipotent creator of moral standards and without him there would be no moral right and wrong. This has the advantage of placing God clearly above morality — it is not an independent yardstick that exists separately of him, but it is under his control. However, it is perhaps the more problematic of the two positions, as suggested by famous biblical narratives such as God's command to Abraham to sacrifice Isaac, or his willingness to allow Satan to test Job almost to death.

While Kierkegaard reached the conclusion that faith is the highest virtue, as exemplified in Abraham's willingness to sacrifice his son for what must have seemed at best a capricious God, at worst a malevolent one, John Habgood exposed the 'nagging doubt' that remains: 'If morality is supposed to be universal, can it really be discounted, even under such extreme pressure from God?'

In modern times, Richard Dawkins, the well-known evolutionary biologist and popular antitheist, has propounded the view that religion leads to evil, likening it to a malignant virus that infects human minds. He dismisses religious faith as 'an indulgence of irrationality that is nourishing extremism, division and terror'. Dawkins draws on a range of evidence, but he is particularly concerned with the beliefs and practices of fundamentalist Islam and evangelical Christianity, which he believes are responsible for misleading education, prejudice and ignorance, inciting fear, and 'child abuse'. Perhaps more importantly, however, he links the events of 9/11 and 7/7 with religiously motivated terrorism: 'Many of us saw religion as harmless nonsense. Beliefs might lack all supporting evidence but, we thought, if people needed a crutch for consolation, where's the harm? September 11th changed all that. Revealed faith is not harmless nonsense; it can be lethally dangerous nonsense.'

In the television documentary *The Root of all Evil?*, Dawkins visited a Hell House Outreach presentation in Colorado. This contained a graphic series of scenes in which homosexuals, women who had abortions, a man who had an affair, and a drunken teenager who was responsible for the death of his girlfriend in a car crash were shown as heading straight for hell. Dawkins talked to Michael Bray, a friend of Paul Hill, the American pastor idolised by the Army of God for his murder of an abortionist, who calmly suggested that it would not be against biblical principles if the state were to execute adulterers. In response, Dawkins quoted Stephen Weinberg: 'Without religion you have good people doing good things, and evil people doing evil things. But for good people to do evil things, it takes religion.'

Unsurprisingly, Dawkins maintains that morality evolves: it is not given by God, nor are we dependent on religion to teach morality. To have morality is part of what it means to be a society and to have learned how to maximise our opportunities in that society — the most important opportunity, of course, being the continuation of the species.

Nevertheless, Dawkins is on shaky ground when he claims that the universe we see is one that has 'no purpose, no evil and no other good, nothing but blind, pitiless indifference...DNA neither knows nor cares. And we dance to its music.' If this is the case, Melvin Tinker argues: 'The logical upshot of this is that the Yorkshire Ripper danced to the music of his DNA'; in other words, he was not accountable for his actions because it was in his DNA, something over which we have little or no control.

Tinker also addresses Dawkins's accusation that religion is harmful. In *The Briefing* he observes: 'He makes a value judgement that extremism and terror are "bad" things, but bad for whom? Not for the terrorists who get their way and pass on their genes.' Finally, Tinker demands that Dawkins be more precise when he talks about religion. Dawkins's sweeping statements suggest that everything he says about religion applies equally to them all, which is as 'intellectually irresponsible as lumping all animals together and saying that what goes for elephants must go for ants'. Rather, it is easy to see that each religion and, within each religion, each denomination, faction or splinter group must be judged on its own terms. In other words, to judge all religious morality on the basis of the extremism of some religious groups is intellectually unsatisfactory.

Although we live in a multicultural world that is, in many ways, highly secular, religious morality is still endemic. For many believers the only good reason to perform a morally good action or to refrain from a morally wrong action is because it conforms to the will of God. We are now far more aware of the diversity of religious traditions and their accompanying moralities, and we can see almost at first hand how powerfully religious morality affects actions that have global significance.

However, A. C. Grayling puts forward an argument for the irrelevance of religion to contemporary morality: 'There is a widespread supposition that a religious ethic...has to be good for individuals and society because it is inherently more likely to make them good. This view is troubling because it is false: religion is precisely the wrong resource for thinking about moral issues in the contemporary world, and indeed subverts moral debate.'

🄴 This is a detailed and well-informed essay that fully meets the requirements of the question. The candidate identifies clearly the two critiques under discussion and shows awareness of many other views by careful use of scholarship and critical evaluation. He/she is stretched by the topic and responds to it at the highest level.

🄴 **You should be ready with specific critiques of the link between religion and morality. Generic claims or sweeping statements will earn only limited credit. This question cannot be answered using just general knowledge or preconceived ideas.**

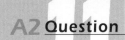

Deontology

Examine the main features of deontology and consider critically
the extent to which it is an adequate ethical theory.   (40 marks)

Deontologists claim that an action or a moral rule is right because of its own nature,
even if it fails to bring about the greatest good. Its moral value lies in the fact that the
action incorporates certain features that are independent of what it brings about — for
instance, because it is a divine command, promise or duty. Deontology is crucially based
on duty (*deontos*) — a moral obligation we have towards another person, a group or
society as a whole, or obligations that are due to them, such as the duty not to steal or
the duty to pay money. Aquinas argued that there are certain duties that are absolute,
including those to ourselves, our families, our fellow citizens, our society and God.
Within this scheme, there are two types of deontology. The first is act deontology, which
allows for different situations to lead to different moral obligations: 'In this situation
I ought to do X.' These may be thought of as *prima facie* duties, which cannot be
anticipated in advance, but to which our intuition will guide us. The second is rule
deontology, which requires the standard of right to depend upon absolute rules, such
as 'We ought always tell the truth.' These rules are permanently valid, regardless of their
outcome.

Deontological constraints or laws are invariably formulated as negatives: 'do not' rather
than 'do'. These constraints help to define what is obligatory or what constitutes our
duty. Deontology therefore consists of two strands: identifying what is permissible and
what is impermissible. That which is permissible, Charles Fried argued, should be the
focus of the deontologist's concerns: 'After having avoided wrong and doing one's duty,
an infinity of choices is left to be made.'

Immanuel Kant is arguably the most famous advocate of modern deontology. He took
an absolutist approach, judging morality by the nature of actions and the purpose of
their agents rather than by the goals they achieved. He believed that the moral
evaluation of actions could not take consequences into consideration. Kant argued that,
since everyone possesses the capacity to reason and has a conscience, it would be
possible for all people to arrive at an understanding of moral truths without the need
for experience. Morality, he claimed, is a priori, not a posteriori, and because reason is
universal, moral reasoning would lead to the same results over and over again.

Kant believed that obedience to the moral law is a 'categorical imperative', that is, an
absolute and unconditional duty on all people to act in a morally correct way. He said
that true morality should not depend on individual likes and dislikes or on abilities,
opportunities or other external circumstances. Obedience to a moral command is an
end in itself. Kant argued that personal preferences are not necessarily wrong, but

cannot be trusted as a reliable guide to what is morally right. Duty is more important and, to this end, he advocated the 'principle of universalisability', which requires people to 'act in such a way that their actions might become a universal law'.

Universalisable principles apply to everyone. In his 'formula of kingdom ends', Kant claimed that every action should be undertaken as if the individual were 'a law-making member of a kingdom of ends'. This should ensure that every individual appreciates the significance of his/her part in establishing moral guidelines and rules. Furthermore, the 'formula of the end in itself' ensures that people are valued for their intrinsic, not instrumental, worth, while the 'formula of autonomy' stresses that a moral action must be genuinely free if it is to be genuinely good.

The main strength of deontology — or the grounds on which the theory may be deemed adequate — is that personal motivation is valued over the consequences of the action. It means that people will act in a way that is worthy and morally right and allows everyone to be considered of equal value and worthy of protection and justice, even if the majority does not benefit. It means that moral absolutes do not change with time or culture — they are beyond fad or fashion and provide clear, objective guidelines for making moral decisions. For those who value an absolutist approach to morality, it limits the potential difficulties of moral decision-making, when even the best intentions can be misguided. For example, reliance on rules laid down by God or society means that errors of moral judgement can simply not be made, even if the outcome of obeying that rule is negative.

However, deontology has several weaknesses or inadequacies. Perhaps the most significant of these is the fact that moral obligations can appear to be arbitrary or inexplicable except by reference to duty. In the same way, deontology provides little help when there are conflicting moral duties — for example, is it right to tell a lie in order to save someone's life? It could be argued that not all things that are universalisable in principle should be universalised in practice — for instance, forbidding people to eat unhealthy foods, or, as has recently become law in the UK, banning smoking in public places. Such rules impose arbitrary and paternalistic limitations on the general public and limit their freedom of choice to act in their own best interests as they see them.

Moreover, Kant argued that what is good to do is what we ought to do and that what is inherently good and intrinsically right is the way in which we ought to behave for the good of all, irrespective of the consequences. Critics of Kant claim that, in saying this, he is committing the naturalistic fallacy — of turning an 'is' into an 'ought'. Furthermore, Kant's view that all moral behaviour should depend on obedience to duty makes no allowances for love, compassion or sympathy in a person's action.

But what does it mean for an ethical theory to be 'adequate'? Presumably, it has to be fit for purpose, practical and flexible enough to be used in any case of moral decision-making. But how far is it possible for any one ethical theory to be fit for purpose in every case where a moral decision is required? For a consequentialist, the absolutism of deontology makes it inherently inadequate, because it cannot offer the flexibility necessary to meet every moral decision with justice. However, for the deontologist, this is the very point. Justice can be served only by ensuring that everyone is subject to the same laws in the same way, and, hence, flexibility leads to injustice, not to fair and equal treatment for all. For the absolutist, therefore, deontology is more than adequate, since whatever its underlying principles, it provides a way of ensuring that morality is equal handed and its expectations are constant.

🄴 The key to gaining top marks in this essay is ensuring that you pay attention to the wording of the question, which this candidate does in the second half of the essay by evaluating the strengths and weaknesses of the theory. The final paragraph tackles convincingly the meaning of 'adequate' in the context of the question. This candidate avoids the common trap of offering a list of strengths and weaknesses without demonstrating how they help to answer the question. He/she focuses on Kantian deontology — the usual approach for this paper — but analysis of other forms of deontology would be equally acceptable. The answer shows sound theoretical knowledge and a good level of understanding and skill.

🄴 **Many candidates choose to answer this type of question, so your essay will need to catch the examiner's eye. Start with a clear definition of deontology and build your answer on theoretical understanding. Avoid a case-study approach, which is typical of lower-grade candidates.**

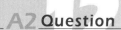
Deontology and virtue ethics

Analyse the key features of deontology and virtue ethics.
To what extent is one a more practical method of resolving
moral dilemmas than the other?   (40 marks)

Aristotle's thinking was influenced by his conviction that all things and all human beings have a purpose or function: a *telos*. A complete explanation of anything would include its final cause or purpose, which is, ultimately, to realise its potential and to fulfil its goal. For human beings, Aristotle maintained that the ultimate goal was human flourishing and developing those characteristics best suited to the realisation of a virtuous human being. His emphasis was not on what people *do*, but on what kind of person they *are*, although *being* a kind person, for example, is essentially accomplished by doing acts of kindness until the habit of being kind is firmly established in a person's character.

Aristotle maintained that the virtues were those qualities that lead to a good life — qualities such as courage, compassion, honesty or justice. A person who aimed to cultivate these qualities was maximising his/her potential for a happy life — a quality of happiness described as *eudaimonia,* which involves being happy and living well. It is of intrinsic value, not a means to an end, and should be desired for its own sake, not only for individuals, but also for the society of which they are members. A person who develops the virtues would be able to act in an integrated way, deriving satisfaction from doing the right thing *because* it is the right thing, and not for any external reasons or goals. They would not act in a particular way either because they *ought* to do so or because they *wanted* to do so, but simply because they had identified the *right* way to act.

For Aristotle, the right way to act is to follow the golden mean. This is a perfect balance between two extremes, such as cowardice and foolhardiness, which are both vices. The golden mean is, of course, courage — a virtue which humans are not born with but which they should cultivate in the way that they might cultivate good health or fitness. People should learn from good role models, train and exercise this virtue, until it becomes an automatic way of living and behaving and part of their character that they can exercise without conscious effort or will. In this way they will become courageous people. This may involve performing courageous acts but, more importantly, their character will acquire the virtue of courage and their actions will be motivated by courage.

Deontological theories of ethics are based on the view that there are certain actions that are right or wrong in themselves, not in the consequences of the action. Wrong actions are wrong per se, and actions that are right are not necessarily those that maximise the good. Deontology, however, identifies those actions that are wrong *even if* they produce predicted or actual good consequences and those that are right simply because of the kind of actions they are. Less commonly, deontology is contrasted with 'aretaic' theories such as virtue ethics, which identify character as the heart of morality.

Immanuel Kant espoused a deontological, or absolutist, approach to ethics, judging morality by examining the nature of actions and the will of their agents rather than the goals they achieved. A primary reason for adopting this approach is that we cannot control consequences because we cannot control the future, however hard we try. While Kant was not unconcerned about the outcome, since he effectively argued a form of the golden rule — 'Do to others what you would have them do to you' (Matthew 7:12) — he insisted that the moral evaluation of actions cannot take consequences into consideration. Furthermore, he believed that since all humans possess reason and a conscience, it would be possible for all people to arrive at an understanding of moral truths independent of experience. Morality is a priori, not a posteriori, and because reason is universal, moral reasoning leads to the same results over and over again.

Kant tried to discover the rational principle that would stand as a categorical imperative for all other ethical judgements. The imperative would have to be categorical rather than hypothetical, since true morality should not depend on individual likes and dislikes or on abilities, opportunities or other external circumstances. Kant's distinction between these two imperatives is vital for his approach. He believed that moral commands are not hypothetical imperatives, which are commands that tell us how to achieve a particular end.

Kant maintained that: 'It is impossible to conceive of anything at all in the world, or even out of it, which can be taken as good without qualification, except a good will.' A good will could be cultivated by use of reason and by working to be rid of those tendencies that make rational decision-making impossible. Kant was concerned with finding *the* categorical imperative that would provide the fundamental moral groundwork for all actions and he found this in the principle of universalisability. He formulated this in his 'formula of the law of nature', which demands that human beings 'act in such a way that their actions might become a universal law'. If the rule or maxim governing our actions cannot be universalised, then it is not morally acceptable, and if you cannot will that everyone follow the same rule, then it is not a moral rule.

Furthermore, Kant's 'formula of kingdom ends' laid down the principle that every action should be undertaken as though the individual were 'a law-making member of a kingdom of ends'. This should ensure that every individual appreciates the significance of his/her part in establishing moral guidelines and rules.

Kant clearly placed great faith in the ability of human beings to work rationally towards such a conclusion and to act freely according to principles. He also placed great value on respect for persons, who, unlike things, are never merely of instrumental value, but of intrinsic value. This means that, although people may be useful, they should not be considered to be means to achieve an end, but to be ends in themselves. This allows deontology to acknowledge human rights and justice as inviolable, something that utilitarianism overlooks. However, in the modern world, ethicists are often more concerned about the need to recognise the differing moral values and standards found in diverse cultures and circumstances. Kant's approach is considered both restrictive and counterintuitive by many, who suggest that it restricts more than it allows. Nevertheless, that which is permissible, Charles Fried argued, should be the focus of the deontologist's concerns: 'After having avoided wrong and doing one's duty, an infinity of choices is left to be made.'

Deontology was given a degree of flexibility by W. D. Ross, who suggested that duties need not be predetermined and inflexible. Ross proposed that we operate on a system of *prima facie* duties that are not prescribed but are known by intuition — they may be duty to family or country, or the duty to show gratitude or ensure justice, but it is only in the situation that we will know which duty is most appropriate.

Virtue ethics underwent a revival in the late twentieth century. Elizabeth Anscombe observed that ethical codes that stress moral absolutes and laws are anachronistic in a society that has effectively abandoned God. She urged a return to a morality that is based on human flourishing. Similarly, Richard Taylor rejected a system of morality based on divine commands and which discouraged people from achieving their potential. Interestingly, he argued that Christianity's emphasis on human equality does not encourage individuals to strive to be great but rather advocates a self-negating humility. Philippa Foot argued that although the virtues could not guarantee happiness, they could help to achieve it, whereas Alastair MacIntyre noted that in moral dilemmas naturalistic theories of ethics are of little value as they are time-consuming and complex. A virtue-based approach to ethics is more realistic and applicable to people's everyday situations.

Virtue ethics is appealing because it can be accommodated by both religious and secular morality. Despite Taylor's observations, Jesus can be held up as a model of the virtuous man, in whom weakness becomes strength and death is transformed into life. It is a simple system based on universal well-being for the individual and the community. In holding up models of virtuous people it does not set unrealistic goals. It is accessible by reference to the real world, since if I describe a person as courageous, the description immediately generates a picture of someone who lives in a particular way and whose way of life recommends itself to the observer. Its greatest strength, perhaps, is that it attempts to link theoretical and practical approaches to ethics and it values moral character that is independent of culture or religion. For this reason I suggest that it offers the more practical method for approaching modern moral dilemmas.

🄴 The trick here is to stay focused on the demands of the question. The candidate achieves this with care, writing almost the same amount on each ethical theory. In the evaluation he/she avoids giving a detailed list of strengths and weaknesses, highlighting only selected points that lead to a conclusion which answers the question set. The candidate makes good use of scholarship, but has a clear understanding of the theories, so he/she avoids the 'death by a thousand scholars' approach.

ℯ **Make sure that you can compare and contrast these theories. Do not assume that you will always be given the option of a question that addresses one ethical theory alone.**

Ethical language

Examine and evaluate the problems raised by ethical language.   (40 marks)

Meta-ethics is the branch of moral philosophy concerned with the question of establishing what it means to say that an action, opinion or attitude is good or bad. Its task is not an easy one, since the word 'good' has many meanings, and most of them are not used in a moral context. Essentially, 'good' is used in relation to a set of standards and is hence a descriptive or factual word. To use the term 'good' prescriptively means that we move from a factual statement to a value judgement.

The important issue is how we use the term 'good' when we are commending or disapproving moral actions. If I say that it would be 'good' to relax the law on assisted suicide or that the Civil Partnerships Act is 'good', in what sense am I using this word? Am I describing a state of affairs that everyone would have to agree with, whether or not it was their preference, or am I expressing a value that is meaningful only to me because it agrees with the way I see the world? In other words, is it realist or anti-realist? A realist view of 'good' leaves us open to few confusions since there will be objective facts that support the evaluation we have given. An anti-realist use, however, is far more problematic, since agreement with the speaker will depend on whether we share in some way their 'form of life'.

Furthermore, moral uses of the term are circular: a good action is excellent or right; the right thing to do is morally good. Thus, employing dictionary definitions of 'good' or 'right' amounts to nothing more than saying: 'What is good is what I believe is good, morally right, excellent, upright...'. By this we see that to say that something is good from a moral perspective does not tell us *why* it is good, only that the speaker considers it to be good.

A key factor in all this is whether ethical dilemmas are subjective or objective, that is whether they are based on personal feelings or on external facts. If a moral opinion is independent of external facts, then it is essentially internal and is to do with how we feel about an ethical issue — so it is subjective. An objective fact, however, is related to how things are in the real world. If moral values are objective, they are similarly true for everyone. Whether morality deals in facts or opinions is the key to whether or not we can place goodness in an objective category, since it is clearly open to many different interpretations.

If morality is objective, then it is cognitive. Cognitive language deals with making propositions about things that can be known and so can be held to be true or false. If it is subjective, then it is non-cognitive and deals with matters that are not simply resolved by establishing whether they are true or false. This is a non-propositional view, which understands language as serving some function other than that of making true/false claims.

Objectivity in ethics is commonly associated with absolutism, which takes the view that ethical principles can be established a priori, that is, without experience. Taking an absolutist approach makes it possible to evaluate moral actions in a critical way, since if an individual or group is not conforming to the recognised absolute standard or law, they can justifiably be condemned for it. However, this depends entirely on societies and individuals coming to an agreement about what constitutes absolute morality, and that it is more than just a matter of personal preference or subjective opinion. So we are back to the initial problem: how can we reach a consensus as to what is 'good' which we can be sure is not subjective opinion, however many people may support it?

The moral relativist argues that we cannot reach a consensus on objective morality because moral values — what is determined as 'good' or 'bad' — are grounded in social custom, and moral judgements are therefore true or false relative to the particular moral framework of the speaker's community. Moral diversity is explained by the fact that moral beliefs are the product of different ways of life and are matters of opinion that vary from culture to culture (cultural relativism) or from person to person and in different situations (moral relativism). Furthermore, our conceptions of morality should be based on how people actually behave (de facto values) rather than an ideal standard of how people should behave (ideal values) because there is no one right or wrong way of behaving.

Ultimately, the implications of moral relativism include accepting that there is no point to moral debate since opposing moral claims are true in an anti-realist sense, relative to the culture from which they emerge. However, moral relativism would allow us to establish morality simply by consulting the community, although there is no room for reform since reformers would be challenging the norms of society.

A key problem in this debate is that naturalistic theories of ethics attempt to define good in terms of something that can be identified in the world or in human nature. G. E. Moore argued that it is not acceptable to 'confuse "Good" with a natural or meta-physical property or holding it to be identical with such a property'. Most importantly, if we say that something *is* the case, we are making a descriptive statement of how things actually are. It describes facts about the world and items in it, whereas a normative or prescriptive statement says that something *ought* to be desired or done. David Hume observed that there is nothing in a descriptive statement that allows us to proceed from what people *actually* do (a factual statement) to making a rule about what people *ought* to do (a value judgement). Moore distinguished between natural facts, which are known through the senses, and moral facts, which are known through intuition. Values are not facts but evaluations of facts. Facts exist independently of human beings and how they feel, but values require humans to exist to make evaluations. Nevertheless, putative facts can be used to support value judgements; hence values are not entirely independent of facts. For example, we may say that abortion is wrong *because* it causes the fetus to suffer, but we still need to provide evidence for the suffering of the fetus for the claim to be objectively true. Moore's position is often called the 'open question argument'. A statement such as 'Anything that brings happiness is good' leads to the question 'Is it good that X leads to happiness?' This is an open question because the answer is 'maybe yes' or 'maybe no'. Hence, it does not increase our moral knowledge about X or about happiness.

Nevertheless, ethical language may still be viewed as prescriptive, even if it does not express a direct command. 'Abortion is wrong' effectively instructs the hearer: 'Do not have an abortion.' 'It is good to give to the poor' encourages the hearer to give. Kantian deontology works on the assumption that reason will guide all people to do their duty and act according to a categorical imperative motivated by good will. While the emotivist argues that moral statements are expressions of feelings, R. M. Hare claimed that they are imperatives that work in the same way as other non-moral commands, such as 'Hurry up'.

However, ethical terms are also descriptive. 'Good' or 'wrong' are used to describe the characteristics of a person or action, but they do not always serve as imperatives. 'The sea is good for swimming' does not prescribe a moral action. Furthermore, even if someone is described as having 'good' qualities, it does not necessarily mean that we are prescribing them for everyone else. Ultimately, it seems that there is no reliable foundation for establishing what is good and, although we have seen several possible answers, it is not decisively resolved.

@ This is a detailed and extensive answer and is the work of a very able candidate. Not only does he/she accurately recall a wealth of detail and reproduce it in the time available, but he/she also answers the question set. There is a pleasing balance between knowledge, understanding and evaluation in this answer, and the candidate demonstrates an ability to respond to whatever question is set on this topic. He/she does not draw a specific conclusion but is confident enough to declare the matter still unresolved. This candidate would be awarded full marks.

@ **Do not think about tackling this question unless you have studied the topic carefully — it is not a matter of common sense. Nevertheless, examiners do enjoy reading well-crafted answers on this less-popular topic.**

Emotivism

Explain what scholars mean when they say that ethical statements are merely expressions of opinion. Assess how far you consider such views to be justified. (40 marks)

Often referred to colloquially as the 'Hurrah!–Boo!' theory, the emotive theory of ethics grew out of the work of the logical positivists and, in particular, A. J. Ayer, who sought to do away with all metaphysical language, which was deemed to be beyond empirical verification and therefore meaningless. This did great damage to religious language, since statements such as 'God exists' were considered meaningless as they deal with metaphysical concepts that cannot be verified or falsified. When applied to ethical language, the logical positivists maintained that ethical statements are not factual propositions as they do not make objectively true claims and there are no observations that can contribute to their verification. The theory of emotivism developed out of this, and its proponents argued that if we make a claim such as 'Abortion is wrong', we are not making a factual claim based on an objective point of reference, but rather a value judgement that can amount to little more than an expression of preference or opinion. When a speaker says 'I don't like abortion', he/she is expressing disapproval of abortion and attempting to persuade others to adopt this preference. On the other hand, if the speaker asserts that 'Euthanasia is good', he/she is expressing approval of euthanasia and is speaking persuasively to the listener. However, there is no factual content to the statement, since we cannot say what facts would contribute to its verification, so it is purely an expression of opinion and as such it provides no further information.

A. J. Ayer (in *Language, Truth and Logic*, 1936) maintained that to identify an action as wrong was to do nothing more than to make some kind of primitive noise. Ethical claims were not designed to make factual claims but to invoke certain emotional responses in the hearer, and so what they mean is less important than what they accomplish. They cannot be justified rationally because all we are doing is trying to encourage other people to agree with our subjective opinions. Ayer suggested that the only useful information that can therefore be gleaned from such claims is the information it conveys about how the speaker or the groups to which he/she belongs think. In this way, Ayer suggested that they are useful providers of psychological and sociological material, but it is never the job of the philosopher to engage in the exchange of such claims. The claims show what is true for the speaker, which is not the same as it being true for everyone. Hence, Ayer suggested that the claim 'You were wrong to steal that money' provides no more information than the claim 'You stole that money'. 'You were wrong to...' only expresses the opinion of the speaker about the action of stealing money — it does not add to our factual knowledge. Thus, it would be no less informative to say 'Stealing money!!!' where, Ayer suggested, 'the quantity and thickness of the exclamation marks indicates a particular tone of horror'.

Rudolph Carnap took a similar view, except that he considered ethical claims to be commands, not expressions of emotive opinion, as did Ayer. If we maintain that ethical claims are commands from God, we are effectively taking this line, while providing a rational reason for them being commands. Bertrand Russell claimed that moral judgements express a wish, while R. B. Braithwaite maintained that they serve to bind the community together. This is a non-cognitive, or anti-realist, view of language, which takes the stance that language does not make factually true claims but serves some other function. If we want religious believers to agree to the same opinion, then to express it as a command from God gives it greater power to convince.

C. L. Stevenson argued that ethical judgements express the speaker's attitude and seek to evoke it in the hearers, but he does allow that our attitudes are based on beliefs that provide reasonable grounds for holding them. We may know that a certain course of action will bring about particular results and thus argue in its favour. Nevertheless, Stevenson does allow that even our most fundamental attitudes may not be rooted in any particular beliefs in which case they cannot be reasoned about. This makes them rather like Hare's 'bliks', which are ways of looking at the world that cannot be verified or falsified, because they are simply opinions.

However, this approach to ethical language and the claims it makes are far too limiting, as was the approach of logical positivism to language in general. It works on the assumption that ethical statements are judged according to the response of the listener and not on the value of the claims themselves, in other words, that the claims have no objective value. If the claim 'Abortion is wrong' says nothing more than 'I don't like abortion', then it is not a claim that can be discussed and evaluated, but this is clearly not the case. If nothing more was being expressed than an unverifiable emotive claim, why is the topic of abortion open to such detailed, scholarly and scientific analysis? The power of the statement 'Abortion is wrong' does not simply lie in how others respond to it — with an equally emotive agreement or disagreement — but in the avenues it opens up for investigation of the claim. If someone maintains that abortion is wrong because he/she has empirical evidence that the fetus feels pain during the procedure, he/she is making a claim that is subject to scientific testing — which has objective, factual value, even if it were proved not to be the case.

Furthermore, if ethical claims were contingent on emotions, they would change as emotions changed. We feel differently about things depending on our experiences and our relationships with others, which are themselves changeable. However, irrespective of our feelings, we tend to hold fast to values that we recognise as having intrinsic value and which set absolute moral standards that apply in any given situation, irrespective of our subjective opinions. Allied to this, if ethical claims simply express subjective, emotive opinions, then they can never be universal claims, and there can be no agreed morality on any issue. Different speakers would express different opinions and there would be no possibility of meaningful debate between them. They would be doing nothing more than expressing an opinion with which they may want others to agree, but without the rational foundations for establishing why they should do so.

Ultimately, even if moral statements are carried by the weight of popular opinion, it does not make that the reason why they are adopted. If the majority of people were of the opinion that euthanasia for anyone over 80 years old was right, it would not make it morally right to carry it out. Equally, if a significant number of people express the view that euthanasia is morally questionable, that opinion is not dismissed as of no real value — it is just the subject of some psychological interest. We recognise that moral views must be and are held for reasons that go beyond opinion, and we trust that the whole process of law making is founded on something more than subjective opinion.

The strength of this essay is its sound grasp of the scholarly issues involved. It is based on thoroughly learned material and makes good use of quotation and direct reference to *Language, Truth and Logic*. It is clear that the candidate understands the issues fully. Although he/she includes a wide range of detail about emotivism, there is plenty of critical evaluation. The closing discussion about euthanasia does not rely on anecdote and is an effective illustration.

You cannot make up an answer to this type of question. Examiners will spot, by the end of the first sentence, whether you know what you are talking about or whether you think this is a common-sense ethics question. If you do not know about Ayer and/or other scholars and their explicit contributions to this debate, do not even consider answering this question.

Natural moral law

Examine and evaluate the view that natural moral law fails to
be a practical ethical theory.   (40 marks)

The principle of natural law is that true law is right reason in agreement with nature,
which can be applied universally and which is unchanging and everlasting. A proponent
of natural moral law theory will maintain that there is one eternal and unchangeable
law valid for all nations and all times, and which is issued by one master and ruler, God.
In his *Summa Theologica*, Aquinas argued that there is a moral code towards which
human beings naturally incline, and this he calls natural moral law. Natural moral law
is thus a deontological system of ethics that predates that of Kant by several centuries,
offering an absolutist foundation for ethical decision-making, consisting of clear moral
guidelines based on a recognisable authority.

Aquinas believed that natural law is accessible through the natural order and that
because it is universal, unchanging and relevant to all circumstances, it provides the
foundation for all moral decision-making and moral knowledge. All human beings can
perceive the natural law, because it is available within the natural world, but only
believers in God acknowledge that it has implications for them beyond the grave and
therefore have a strong sense of why it should be followed.

Natural law draws its inspiration from the Bible as well as from the common reason
of mankind. In Romans 1–3, Paul argued that the moral law of God is evident from the
nature of humans and the world: 'Ever since the creation of the world his invisible
nature, namely, his eternal power and deity has been clearly perceived in the things that
have been made' (Romans 1:20). Paul maintained that since natural moral law is so
clearly evident in the universe, sinful humans have no excuse for wrongdoing. For
example, in Matthew 19:3–9, Jesus observes that the divorce law in the Torah was a
concession to the sinful nature of humans and not what God had originally intended
in the order of creation, but natural moral knowledge should make it clear that divorce
is wrong. Hence, returning to foundational principles, he forbids divorce, which had
been permitted by the Law of Moses, on all grounds except unfaithfulness. This natural
law was made known to humans through four channels: eternal law — God's will and
wisdom; divine law — God's will and wisdom is given in scripture and through the
church; natural law — by which God's law is known in humans; and human law —
which is derived from God.

The principle of natural law depends on establishing the purpose of human life, and
Aquinas maintained that purpose is to live, reproduce, learn, worship God and order
society. All things must operate in accordance with these principles to which humans
are naturally inclined. God gives humans reason to accomplish these purposes whether

they believe in him or not. The natural law, instituted by God, gives humans the opportunity to work towards the good in all things. Paul recognised, however, that this is not always possible, 'since all have sinned and fallen short of the glory of God' (Romans 3:23). Humans will fall short of God's best for them because this is a fallen world and they violated the perfect relationship with God and the natural order that was instituted at the creation. Nevertheless, the rational person will desire communication with God and will act to accomplish it, despite the limitations of humanity. Any action that takes humanity closer to this goal is good, and any action that takes it further away is wrong. Aquinas maintained that every individual also has a purpose specific to him/her, which will fulfil the skills and talents given to him/her by God. While the goal of a relationship with God is open to all, other goals are only open to some.

Natural law theory could be said to be strong because it is a simple, universal guide for judging the moral value of human actions, and the purposes that Aquinas proposed for human existence are those that are common to all people. Moral law is made accessible by our reason, and it makes God's reason accessible to a believer because humans and God share the same rationality. Upholders of naturalism would argue that the law ought to reflect the universal set of morals that all people can discern from the universe in this way. It provides a straightforward set of rules for making moral decisions, claiming that all we need to do is look at the evidence of the natural world and apply our reason, and we will come to the right conclusion. Nature cannot guide us wrongly.

However, Aquinas made certain assumptions that may no longer seem practical or relevant in the twenty-first century. He assumed that all men seek to worship God, and many would see this as artificial, illusory and dangerous, not natural. If belief in God grows out of psychological or sociological needs or functions, then it is not natural in the sense that Aquinas intended. The moral reasoning that humans acquire on the basis of that belief serves or reinforces the society in which they live or their own psychological needs. Furthermore, Aquinas gave pride of place to reproduction as one of the common, universal aims of humans. In doing so he opened up thorny issues for homosexuals and for those who are biologically incapable of having children, let alone those who for personal reasons choose not to do so, such as those who dedicate themselves to celibacy for religious purposes.

Aquinas thought of every individual and every part of every individual as having a particular function to fulfil. This goes against the 'portfolio' thinking of modern times by which we recognise the variety of functions that people can fulfil. Rather, it is a concept borrowed from the thinking of ancient Greek philosophy, which maintained that a society in which every individual served a single purpose is an ordered and efficient one. Natural law theory allows no room for situationism, relativism, consequentialism or individualism. It is highly prescriptive and does not permit any flexibility, which is more in keeping with modern ethical thinking.

Finally, Aquinas committed the naturalistic fallacy: he maintained that moral law comes from God (a matter of fact in his thinking) and therefore we ought to obey it (a value judgement). This is an example of the 'is–ought' gap in moral thinking: just because we maintain that something is a matter of fact does not make it a matter of value. Even if moral law comes from God, this does not mean that everyone will agree that we ought to obey it.

Proportionalism, associated particularly with Bernard Hoose and Richard McCormick, works within the framework of natural law, but it does not insist on preserving a static, inflexible and absolutist interpretation if a greater good is served by laying it aside. Aquinas's teaching does allow for some degree of proportionalism. For example, he allowed that if a man is starving, it is acceptable to steal rather than let him die of hunger. A proportionalist may argue that the best we can aim for is a theology of compromise that recognises that since we live in a fallen world (affected by original sin), the best that human beings can strive towards is a moral compromise, not moral perfection. Proportionalism may be seen to be more compassionate than a strict application of natural law. However, it could be said to allow too much freedom to decide what is proportionately good and permits the rejection of authoritarian moral codes such as those laid down by the Roman Catholic Church. Furthermore, proportionalism may be thought to be utilitarianism under another guise, since it takes into account the outcome of an action, not its intrinsic worth.

It is easy to write down all you know about natural moral law, but less easy to apply that information correctly in answering an exam question. This candidate avoids a tedious list of case studies when illustrating the problem of relating the theory to modern moral problems. Instead he/she relates it clearly to theoretical issues, which is a more rigorous and academic approach. Furthermore, the candidate shows knowledge and understanding of modern approaches to natural moral law, which gives the essay a pleasing and unexpected lift.

You should try to impress the examiners with a wider range of knowledge than they would expect from most candidates. This is a popular topic, so you must aim to make your essay unique. Be aware too that you might have to combine discussion of this ethical theory with deontology or virtue ethics, so do not be put off if you are not asked to write about natural moral law on its own.

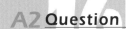

Selected problem in ethics

Examine *either* authority *or* law and punishment. Assess the contribution made to the issue chosen by *either* objectivity *or* subjectivity.   (40 marks)

Jeremy Bentham observed that 'All punishment is mischief...all punishment, in itself, is evil'. Nevertheless, punishments are given to ensure that laws are obeyed. Punishment is the intentional infliction of pain or suffering by a legitimate authority on those who have breached its laws. In the UK, the main forms of punishment are imprisonment, fines and community services orders, depending on the severity of the crime. Charles Colson observes that: 'The primary purpose of criminal justice is to preserve order with the minimum infraction of individual liberty. Accomplishing this requires a system of law that people can agree on and that therefore possesses not just power but authority.'

An objective view of punishment is based on the view that there are absolute punishments designed to apply to all crimes of a particular type and that no just system of punishment can permit any degree of relativism or subjectivity. Punishment is therefore an essential part of a system that takes seriously the notions of justice, authority and law. However, the exact purpose of punishment needs to be clear and it is the state's duty to ensure that forms of punishment do not infringe the human rights of the offender. From an objective perspective, punishment must treat offenders and their rights equally, just as it should protect the rights of the victim. Punishment should therefore be humane and proportional to and respectful of the equality and dignity of all human beings.

There are several purposes to punishment: deterrence, reform/rehabilitation, protection, vindication of the law and retribution. The first four purpose may be justified on utilitarian grounds — punishment is a means of minimising suffering and protecting society. The punishment imposed on one person allows many others to live in safety. The fifth purpose, retribution, is commonly defended on the grounds of natural justice. People naturally tend to want revenge if they are wronged. Unlimited revenge would lead to anarchy, so the state limits and controls the amount of revenge that is taken. Natural justice is objective in the way that natural rights are and belong to all people irrespective of their situation, culture or circumstances.

C. S. Lewis argued that punishment based on deserts is part of natural law. This is the retributive theory of punishment found in the work of Kant, a deontological absolutist. For Lewis, desert is the only proper basis for deciding what happens to criminals. Although deterrence and rehabilitation sound merciful, the criminal is losing the protection of natural law, which ensures that he/she is punished only so far as is just, and instead is at the mercy of apparent experts who, by permission of the state, can do whatever they want to the criminal to make him/her act and behave as they see fit.

Hence, punishment is not objective, but subjective, and depends on the whim of those who carry it out.

However, for the objectivist, it is of fundamental importance that an offender must have committed a crime as an autonomous moral agent. In looking at the evidence, a court has to decide not only what happened and whether the accused person intended to commit the crime, but also whether the person intended to commit an illegal act. This means that limits must be placed on the punishment of those who are not free moral agents — for example, those who commit crimes while suffering from mental illness. This is not run-away subjectivity but a means by which the objective application of the law can be ensured.

Most punishments are a mixture of all these aspects. For example, putting an offender in prison acts as deterrence, retribution and protection and, with the aid of education and guidance while in prison, offenders can be reformed. However, in the UK, nearly half of all prisoners re-offend after release and are sent back to prison. So if imprisonment is intended as an objective means of dealing with offences, in many ways it fails since its value is not recognised by all those who are subject to it.

The most extreme form of punishment favoured by absolutist views of punishment is capital punishment, or execution. In the UK, the death penalty was abolished in 1965 by the Murder (Abolition of the Death Penalty) Act and, under the European Convention on Human Rights, the death penalty is restricted to times of national emergency. Other nations, including some states of the USA, still have the death penalty. It is estimated that there is one legal execution somewhere in the world nearly every day. China is the world's leader in capital deaths.

Ethical theorists have long debated whether the death penalty is an effective punishment. Some argue that there is an absolute right to life and that the taking of a human life by another human being can never be justified. This is a categorical imperative, for it is based not on the nature of the crime, or the needs of society. It stems from the overriding principle of the value of human life, which is of objective and eternal value — it does not depend on opinion or personal preference.

Others take a utilitarian approach, claiming that the loss of one criminal's life is balanced against the cost to society of keeping that person in prison for life, or the potential suffering that could result if that person were released from prison and re-offended. This allows for a relative approach to punishment and permits the taking of life in these exceptional circumstances. However, recent studies in the USA have suggested that it costs up to six times more to execute prisoners than it does to keep them in prison for life, since the appeals process can take many years of expensive legal argument. Some people support capital punishment because the death penalty is thought to act as a deterrent to those thinking of committing a serious crime. It means that society can rid itself of its most dangerous and undesirable citizens and provides the ultimate revenge and compensation for taking the life of another. Execution gives the victim's family a sense of retribution. Nevertheless, some may argue that forgiveness is a more important absolute, and that victims' loved ones should be encouraged to forgive offenders rather than take satisfaction in their deaths.

However, in countries where the death penalty is enforced, the number of murders does not seem to drop — execution is, apparently, no deterrent. Many innocent people have been wrongly executed. Terrorists who are executed can become martyrs and this encourages more terrorism. Ultimately, many opponents argue that human life is important, even sacred, and should not be taken away under any circumstances. However, some may argue that prisoners should be allowed to choose execution instead of life imprisonment and that those in prison for life have a 'right to die'.

Finally, in his survey of the plight of prisoners in the USA and UK, Charles Colson argues for restorative or relational justice. He claims that the system of punishment has failed and that prisons are filled with many people who are not dangerous to society and are '...often hardened in their criminal disposition because of their experience'. Colson advocates a radical overhaul of the system of justice and imprisonment to allow the criminal to be reformed and reintegrated into the community: '...a criminal justice system that not only provides just deserts, but provides redemption as well — that recovers the wholeness of the community shattered by crime, a justice that restores'. In some ways this promotes an objective view of justice, but it is not the objectivity of revenge or retribution. It encourages the view that restoration and healing are the ultimate goal to which society as a whole should aim.

e Candidates often do not know how to best tackle this topic, but this answer takes the sensible approach of blending the evaluative demand of the question with knowledge and understanding of punishment. It reads fluently and shows that the candidate can use the material confidently. Some useful quotations illustrate the key points, and the conclusion makes good use of modern scholarship. The candidate does not rely just on GCSE material when discussing the purposes of punishment.

e **Do not try to learn everything about all these related ideas in the specification. Simply target those that you want to write about in the exam. There will always be sufficient choice and, inevitably, the concepts overlap. Note that this candidate includes ideas about relativism or subjectivism in punishment even though he/she focuses on objectivity.**

The purpose of Luke's Gospel

'The purpose of the Gospel was to bring the good news of universal salvation.' With reference to the views of scholars, examine and consider critically this view of the purpose of the author of Luke's Gospel.

(40 marks)

There are differing opinions among scholars about the exact purpose of the author of Luke's Gospel, since it is both a historical account and a theological discourse on the life and teaching of Jesus Christ, as Luke himself stated: 'Therefore, since I myself have carefully investigated everything from the beginning, it seemed good also to me to write an orderly account for you, so that you may know the certainty of the things you have been taught' (1:3–4).

It was Hanz Conzelmann, in _The Theology of St Luke_, who suggested that Luke had written a gospel concerned with universal salvation. He argued that Luke's historical and geographical knowledge was often inaccurate, but the important theme was that of Christ at the centre of God's plan of salvation. Moreover, Luke's message was not aimed just at the Jews. They refused to acknowledge Jesus, so, through the grace of God, salvation is now for everyone because God's love is universal. In _Luke: Historian and Theologian_, I. H. Marshall observed: '…the idea of salvation supplies the key to the theology of Luke.'

This theme was taken up by Leon Morris, who said that Luke offered a universal message of salvation for all — Gentiles, women, social outcasts, the sick and the poor — that God is at work in human affairs and that, through Christ, salvation is available to all in the present time, when 'all mankind will see God's salvation' (3:6). Morris claimed: 'Luke emphasises that salvation has become present in Christ…In Jesus the time of salvation has come.'

The universal message of salvation is emphasised by the sayings of Jesus, such as: 'Blessed are you who are poor, for yours is the kingdom of God' (6:20). Luke also frequently refers to the Samaritans (9:51–54, 10:30–37) and, most notably, to the Gentiles. He refers to Christ as '…a light for revelation to the Gentiles' (2:32) and emphasises that Jesus's great commission to the disciples was that the Gospel should be '…preached in his name to all nations' (24:47). Indeed, in the incident involving the centurion, G. B. Caird observed: '…the highest praise ever uttered by Jesus was addressed to a Gentile.'

Luke shows that all are loved by God, even the most wretched. In _Essays on New Testament Themes_, Ernst Käsemann writes: 'A particular feature of Luke's narrative which can shed light on the nature of the community and society for whom he writes is the concern for the weak and downtrodden, the sinners, and the despised.' Thus, the Magnificat tells how God has 'lifted up the humble. He has filled the hungry with good things' (1:52–53). In the same way, the woman who lost a coin (15:8), the shepherd who seeks the lost sheep (15:3) and the parable of the lost son (15:11–32) show that God's love is universal and that all are included. In *Not Ashamed of the Gospel,* Morna Hooker writes: 'We will not be surprised, later in the Gospel, to find Jesus declaring that he has come to seek out and save the lost; nor will we be surprised to learn that the humble and the outcast find a place in the Kingdom of God, while the arrogant and mighty are excluded.'

Universal salvation is shown by the Gospel in the way that God is seen to carry out his plan through the lives of ordinary people, particularly women. Several are mentioned, including Mary (Jesus's mother), Elizabeth, Anna, Martha and Mary, and Mary Magdalene. Women also feature heavily in incidents such as the widow of Nain (7:11) and the sinful woman (7:37), as well as in the parables of the lost coin (15:8) and the persistent widow (18:1). Leon Morris comments: 'An important part of God's concern for people is that it is manifested towards groups not highly esteemed in first century society: women, children, the poor, the disreputable...even the little people matter to God.'

However, scholars have argued that the message of universal salvation may not have been the only purpose of the author of the Gospel. In *Saint Luke,* G. B. Caird believed that Luke's main purpose in writing the Gospel was as an apologia to the Romans. He claimed that Luke wrote his Gospel so that the Romans would understand that Christianity was not a threat to them: 'His story will tell how Christ turned his back on political revolution in the realm of ideas and values...a figure of nobility, grace and charm, able to reproduce these same qualities in the lives of his followers and to raise the decency and dignity even of the outcasts.'

Meanwhile, F. C. Grant in *Current Issues in New Testament Interpretation* finds a different purpose, namely that Luke intended 'to clear up points of misunderstanding or misrepresentation which had arisen in the pagan world'. For Morna Hooker, the main purpose of Luke was to show that Christ's death was the culmination of God's love and righteousness: 'Jesus's death, then, is seen by Luke, as a new Exodus, a great redemptive act.'

Yet this is, in a real sense, intertwined with the theme of universal salvation. Luke's message is that God's love reaches out to all who are willing to hear and receive it. Luke does not speak of Christ's death on the cross as an act of triumph but as the way to salvation. Leon Morris explains that 'Luke looks for the coming of the End when the salvation of which he writes will reach its consummation'.

The message does not end with Christ's death — it goes on through the resurrection, According to I. H. Marshall, this is 'the crucial event in Luke's salvation history'. More than this, for Luke, it goes on in the promise of the Holy Spirit that is given by the risen Christ (24:49) to the disciples to enable them to preach the message: '...one of Luke's great emphases is the Holy Spirit...God's love is seen in the Spirit who enters and empowers and guides the followers of Jesus' (Leon Morris).

e This essay is worth an A grade because it offers clear knowledge and understanding of the issues involved and provides a range of examples, backed up with evidence and scholarship. The candidate refers to a wide range of texts and includes scholarly viewpoints that support the material from the Gospel itself. Arguments are expressed clearly and themes are developed fluently with comprehensive use of technical language and a thorough discussion of the issues. Key points are examined and discussed, and arguments are viewed from both sides and backed up with scholarship and textual evidence. The conclusion is thought-provoking and shows a well-balanced understanding, demonstrating the depth of theological study that this candidate has achieved.

e **You should try to blend scholarship and textual knowledge in such an essay. Lists of scholars and their views alone are tedious and do not show that you have absorbed the biblical text; textual material needs to be put into a scholarly context.**

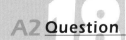
The kingdom of God in Luke's Gospel

Examine and consider critically the views of scholars concerning
Jesus's teaching on the kingdom of God in Luke's Gospel.   (40 marks)

'I must preach the good news of the kingdom of God...because that is why I was sent'
(Luke 4:43).

Luke mentions God's kingdom 35 times in his Gospel. He refers to the ways in which
God acts and intervenes in human history to establish his rule. In a real sense, it is God's
work that Luke refers to, rather than to a kingdom. The most important part of this
message is that it is through Jesus Christ that the kingdom will be established.
I. H. Marshall, in *Luke: Historian and Theologian*, observes: 'Luke associates the coming
of the kingdom not only with the preaching but also with the mighty works of Jesus
which are signs of the activity of God. The coming of the kingdom is firmly tied historically with the ministry of Jesus.'

From the beginning of his Gospel, Luke portrays Christ as the king and ruler of the
kingdom that will last forever: 'He will be great and be called the Son of the Most
High...he will reign over the house of Jacob forever; his kingdom will never end'
(1:32–33). Yet scholars are divided about the exact meaning of Jesus's teaching
concerning the kingdom. Some, like E. Schweizer, believe that Jesus was teaching that
the kingdom would come immediately. Others, such as C. H. Dodd, argue that the
kingdom was already present in the person and ministry of Jesus. This is called 'realised
eschatology'. Dodd cites such references as '...the kingdom of God has come to you'
(11:20) and '...the kingdom of God is within you' (17:21). However, E. P. Sanders
suggests that Jesus was talking about a kingdom that would come about in the distant
future. Certainly, Luke is far from clear on this. In 10:9, Jesus says '...the kingdom of
God is near', yet the parable of the ten minas (19:12–27) and the conversation with
the criminal on the cross imply that the kingdom is in the future: 'Jesus, remember me
when you come into your kingdom' (23:42). I. H. Marshall suggests that the overall
message contains all these aspects: 'Jesus is the destined king during His earthly ministry
and assumes His kingly throne at His ascension.'

Not only does Luke highlight the coming of the kingdom through the miracles of Jesus,
which are signs of God's activity in the world, but also, and perhaps more significantly,
through the preaching of Jesus. Thus, Jesus makes it clear that the kingdom of God is
for the poor (6:20) and those who are least on Earth (7:28; 13:30; 14:14) and he issues
a warning against those who have worldly wealth and do not recognise their spiritual

needs (18:25, 29). The parable of the sower highlights the fact that only those who hear the message of the kingdom with faith and a responsive heart will inherit it: 'But the seed on good soil stands for those with a noble and good heart, who hear the word, retain it, and by persevering produce a crop' (8:15). Leon Morris, in *Luke*, notes: 'Parables both reveal and conceal truth: they reveal it to the genuine seeker who will take the trouble to dig beneath the surface and discover the meaning, but they conceal it from him who is content simply to listen to the story.'

Similarly, the parable of the great banquet uses the image of the messianic banquet to suggest that those who enter the kingdom will do so by God's invitation: 'Blessed is the man who will eat at the feast in the kingdom of God' (14:15). God's kingdom will not be given to those who are important by human standards — it is the poor and humble who will receive it first. Those who turn their backs on God's invitation will lose out. Leon Morris notes: 'The story of the banquet emphasises the truth that people are saved by responding to God's invitation, not by their own effort, whereas if they are lost it is by their own fault.'

Perhaps the clearest illustration of this comes in the parables of the lost. These stories highlight a recurring theme in Luke's Gospel, that of seeking God and finding salvation. God does not simply wait for people; he helps them to find him and then rejoices as a lost sinner is found. Thus, in the parable of the lost sheep, Jesus says: 'There will be more rejoicing in heaven over one sinner who repents than over ninety-nine righteous persons who do not need to repent' (15:7). Similarly, the parable of the lost son highlights God's forgiving love. He welcomes the sinner back and ignores the complaints of the other son. The kingdom is about showing love to repentant sinners and welcoming all those who come to God in faith and humility.

There is also an eschatological aspect to the kingdom. Christ is shown as the fulfilment of Old Testament scriptures and lies at the heart of God's plan for salvation. Thus, Jesus is shown to fulfil the prophecies of Isaiah to preach 'good news to the poor' (4:18), give 'recovery of sight for the blind' (4:18) and release 'the oppressed' (4:18). Yet alongside these are more ominous references to the end of things, when 'Jerusalem will be trampled on by the Gentiles' (21:24) before humanity will see 'the Son of Man coming in a cloud with power and great glory' (21:27). It is then that the parousia or Second Coming of Christ will usher in the kingdom in its fullness: '...the Son of Man will come at an hour when you do not expect him' (12:40). Luke suggests that the coming of the kingdom will be a time of joy and salvation. Leon Morris writes: '...he looks for the coming of the End when the salvation of which he writes will reach its consummation'.

Although the teachings on the kingdom are uncertain, I. H. Marshall suggests that, whenever the kingdom comes, it is a present reality and relevant for the life of all people: 'While Luke retains the hope of the future coming of the kingdom, he also stresses the presence of the kingdom as a reality in the ministry of Jesus.'

e This essay offers a full and thorough exposition of the topic, backed up by a range of textual and background evidence supported by scholarship. The textual narrative is used to provide evidence and a detailed discussion of the key points. The views of scholars are used to clarify the arguments, and themes are developed fluently and clearly with good use of technical language. The teachings of Judaism are contrasted with the teaching of Jesus, particularly the notion that Jesus's teaching was very much for the present and the future. This kind of answer shows examiners how well you understand the issues. The candidate does more than just tell the parables and uses a skilful blend of textual knowledge with scholarship and relevant quotations to amplify the main points. Moreover, he/she does not fall into the trap of giving unnecessary information. There is a strong formula in the main paragraphs, where textual narrative and scholarship are used to balance and expand the main points. The conclusion is balanced and well argued, making this an excellent grade-A response.

e **The question tells you clearly what you are required to do. You have to offer the views of scholars on the teaching of Jesus on the kingdom of God in Luke's Gospel. It will not do to give just textual information, particularly if it is only half-remembered from GCSE. Do not tackle this question unless you have prepared for its specific demands.**

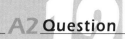

Conflict in Luke's Gospel

'According to Luke's Gospel, the religious and political authorities came into conflict with Jesus because they were afraid of him.' Examine and evaluate this claim.

(40 marks)

Jesus came into conflict with the religious authorities during his ministry and with the political authorities at his trial. The conflict came about because the authorities were afraid of Jesus — they believed that he posed a threat to Judaism and to the peace of Israel. For the religious authorities, Jesus was a challenge to the traditional system of Jewish law, worship and ritual. Crucially, he claimed to be the Son of Man, with a unique relationship with God — one that the religious authorities could not accept or understand. They saw Jesus as a false prophet, which meant that, under the Law of Moses, he was punishable by death: 'If a prophet appears among you and announces to you a miraculous sign or wonder, and if that sign or wonder of which he has spoken takes place, and he says "Let us follow other gods"...you must not follow the words of that prophet. The Lord is testing you to find out whether you love him with all your heart and with all your soul...that prophet must be put to death' (Deuteronomy 13:1–5).

The Romans were the political authorities. They wanted two things: to collect taxes and to maintain the nation in a state of peace. They were afraid of anyone who was a threat to that peace, so they required that the religious authorities dealt firmly with any potential troublemakers.

Jesus became a cause for concern to the religious authorities because they regarded his teaching as a threat to their own position and he was not afraid to challenge their observation of the law: 'Now then, you Pharisees clean the outside of the cup and dish, but inside you are full of greed and wickedness. You foolish people!' (Luke 11:39). This simmering conflict was finally ignited when Jesus entered Jerusalem in triumph, riding a donkey in fulfilment of prophecy. The people were looking for a king. They had seen Jesus perform miraculous works and believed it could be him: 'Shout, Daughter of Jerusalem! See, your king comes to you, righteous and having salvation, gentle and riding on a donkey' (Zechariah 9:9).

Then Jesus entered the Temple area, where he found market traders selling animals for sacrifice and changing money, making a profit at the expense of the worshippers. The religious authorities allowed this to happen, so Jesus became angry and drove the traders out, quoting from the prophecy of Isaiah 56:7: '"It is written," he said to them, "My house will be 'a house of prayer', but you have made it 'a den of robbers'"' (19:46). By this action, Jesus was challenging the religious authorities in the heart of Judaism itself, the Temple. Infuriated and afraid of what he might do next, they decided to kill him. Ellis Rivkin observes: 'It was not easy for the authorities to decide what to do about charismatic leaders who preached no violence and built no revolutionary organisations, but rather urged the people to repent and to wait for the coming of God's kingdom. Were these charismatics harmless preachers, or were they troublemakers?'

The Jewish authorities tried to trick Jesus into condemning himself by asking him where his authority came from. Jesus refused to answer them because they were unable to say where John the Baptist's authority to baptise came from. Leon Morris points out: 'Throughout the whole of the four Gospels it is clear that he is very conscious of possessing the highest authority. But he will not speak about it to men who will not answer a plain question to which they know the answer.'

When this trick failed, the religious authorities tried to trap Jesus into making a treasonable statement by asking whether he thought Jews should pay Roman taxes. Jesus's reply did not help them: 'Then give to Caesar what is Caesar's, and to God what is God's' (20:25). Jesus warned the people against the religious authorities, saying that they enjoyed the luxury of their position and made a false display of being holy and righteous: 'Beware of the teachers of the law. They like to walk around in flowing robes and love to be greeted in the market places and have the most important seats in the synagogues' (20:46).

As the Passover approached, the religious authorities decided to take action against Jesus because they 'were afraid of the people' (22:2). They were afraid to arrest him in daylight and so they seized him at night: 'But this is your hour — when darkness reigns' (22:53). Jesus was taken to the high priest and then before the Sanhedrin. No accusations were made against him, nor were any witnesses called, and proper trial procedures were not observed. Jesus did not answer their questions directly, for he knew that they would not believe him: 'The Son of Man must suffer many things and be rejected by the elders, chief priests and teachers of the law, and he must be killed and on the third day be raised to life' (9:22).

The religious authorities asked the crucial question: 'Are you then the Son of God?' (22:70). To claim to be the Son of God was a blasphemy under the Law of Moses, punishable by death. Jesus answered: 'You are right in saying I am' (22:70) and the Sanhedrin condemned him to death: 'A prophet who presumes to speak in my name anything I have not commanded him to say...must be put to death' (Deuteronomy 18:20). Only the Romans, as the political authority, could pass the death sentence or *ius gladii*. So the Sanhedrin brought Jesus before Pilate. Blasphemy was not a crime in Roman law, so the Jews accused Jesus of crimes that the Romans would find serious: 'subverting our nation' (23:2), opposing the payment of taxes to Caesar and claiming to be 'Christ, a king' (23:2).

Pilate was uncomfortable with the whole proceeding. He asked Jesus whether he was the King of the Jews, and declared that he found no charge against him. Pilate sent Jesus to Herod, who also found Jesus to be innocent of any crime. Pilate wanted to release

Jesus, but the crowd shouted for him to release a murderer called Barabbas. Ellis Rivkin observes: 'Had there been no Roman imperial system, Jesus would have faced the buffetings of strong words, the batterings of skilfully aimed proof texts, and the ridicule of both Sadducees and Scribes-Pharisees, but he would have stood no trial, been affixed to no cross.'

Although Pilate felt that Jesus had done nothing wrong, Pilate condemned him to death because he was afraid, not of Jesus, but of what the religious authorities and the crowd might do. Leon Morris writes: 'It was not Pilate or his Romans who called for Jesus's execution: it was the Jewish chief priests and their followers.'

This essay has a positive introduction that sets the scene. The candidate identifies the key issues and characters, making use of religious terms and textual context and background. The reference to the law in Deuteronomy is crucial to the whole answer yet most candidates fail to mention it. The candidate uses the Old Testament background material successfully — the meaning and interpretation of these words lie at the very heart of the conflict. He/she also addresses the issues clearly and directly, using scholarly sources supported by textual evidence. There is also useful evaluation of the complex issues, motives and arguments, as well as good use of technical language. This is a well-informed and clear analysis of the issues and a detailed coverage of the fears of the religious authorities, supported by textual evidence and the views of scholars. The conclusion is concise. The candidate offers a modern alternative to traditional viewpoints and uses scholarly sources to back up his/her evaluation of the problem in a reasoned way. The final quotation is direct, powerful and challenging — an excellent way to end a thought-provoking essay.

Do not rely on a narrative approach based on an endless retelling of Jesus's conflicts with the Pharisees, especially the Sabbath controversies — the issue is deeper than this, as is shown by the high level of scholarship in this answer.

The crucifixion and resurrection in Luke's Gospel

Examine the religious symbolism contained in the account of the crucifixion in Luke's Gospel. To what extent was the resurrection an important aspect of Jesus's ministry? (40 marks)

In the crucifixion narrative, Luke uses many of the themes and symbols from earlier in the Gospel. In particular, the narratives emphasise both the innocence of Jesus and the hope of salvation that comes from his death. Luke highlights Jesus's innocence and it is clear he believes that it is the Jewish religious authorities, rather than Pilate, who bear the final responsibility for the death of Jesus. He writes of how '...they led him away' (23:26) and that all condemned prisoners were forced to walk through the city streets to Golgotha, facing the abuse and anger of the citizens on the way. Jesus tells those who mourn him: '...do not weep for me; weep for yourselves and for your children' (23:28).

Jesus is crucified along with 'two other men, both criminals' (23:32). Luke deliberately uses this expression to distinguish them from Jesus, who is not a criminal. This fulfils the prophecy of Isaiah 53:9: 'He was assigned a grave with the wicked' and of 53:12: '...numbered with transgressors'. Jesus utters the famous words of forgiveness (not found in the earliest manuscripts of the Gospel) against those who have sought his death: 'Father, forgive them, for they do not know what they are doing' (23:34). Jesus is nailed to the cross and any Jew dying in this way was denied the right to enter heaven: '...anyone who is hung on a tree is under God's curse' (Deuteronomy 21:23). He was offered wine-vinegar to drink as a painkiller. Possibly this drink is symbolic of the sour wine that represents Judaism, as opposed to the rich wine that is the blood of Christ. The soldiers draw lots for Jesus's clothes, in fulfilment of the prophecy written in Psalm 22:16–18: 'A band of evil men has encircled me, they have pierced my hands and feet...They divided my garments among them and cast lots for my clothing.' Above Jesus is a notice that reads: 'This is the King of the Jews' (23:38), perhaps intended as a taunt by Pilate against those who have sought the death of their king.

One of the two criminals knows that Jesus is innocent. He asks Jesus to remember him when he comes into his kingdom and Jesus's reply highlights the nature of God's love and forgiveness: 'Today you will be with me in paradise' (23:43). Moran Hooker observes: 'Jesus's response is an indication of the salvation and forgiveness which he offers to those who repent.' This incident continues the Gospel's theme of seeking and saving the lost. Frank Matera, in *Passion Narratives and Gospel Theologies*, wrote: 'Luke portrays Jesus as the Messiah who refuses to save himself, but continues to save others even at the moment of death.'

Darkness covers the whole land from the sixth hour (12 noon) and lasts until the ninth hour (3 p.m.). In the Old Testament, darkness symbolised the anger of God: 'The sun will be turned into darkness...before the coming of the great and dreadful day of the Lord' (Joel 2:31). At the ninth hour (3 p.m.) the curtain in the Temple was torn in two. This is profoundly symbolic. The most sacred part of the Temple was called the Holy of Holies and it was protected by a great curtain. It was the place of the presence of God and the curtain formed a barrier between God and his people. The tearing of the curtain, on the death of Jesus, meant that the barrier was removed, and access to God — and to salvation — was available to all.

Jesus's last words are 'Father, into your hands I commit my spirit' (23:46). Jesus does not die alone, but in triumph and in the hands of his Father. Morna Hooker comments: '...to human eyes, what has happened looks like utter disaster, but to the eyes of faith it is a cause for praising God.'

Joseph of Arimathea buried the body of Jesus in a tomb cut out of rock in accordance with Isaiah's prophecy of the suffering servant being 'with the rich in his death' (53:9). Joseph laid Jesus to rest before the beginning of the Sabbath, as required by the Law of Moses: 'If a man guilty of a capital offence is put to death and his body is hung on a tree...be sure to bury him that same day' (Deuteronomy 21:22–23). The resurrection was an important part of the Gospel because it marked the completion of God's saving work. The empty tomb was the proof of the reality of the resurrection and this confirmed that Jesus Christ truly was the Son of God and that his teachings were true. This enabled the disciples to go out into the world and preach the Gospel: 'This is what is written; the Christ will suffer and rise from the dead on the third day and repentance and forgiveness of sins will be preached in his name to all nations, beginning at Jerusalem. You are my witnesses of these things' (24:46–48). Moreover, as John Drane noted, the resurrection broke down the barrier between God and humanity and marked the dawning of a new age: 'Without the resurrection, the cross might have been an interesting theological talking point, but would have been powerless to have any lasting effect on the lives of ordinary people.'

However, some scholars have questioned the importance of the resurrection, highlighting the fact that the author gives it little space and that, possibly, it was symbolic rather than real, to encourage the faith of the early believers. Morna Hooker writes: 'Luke freely acknowledges the difficulty of believing in the truth of the resurrection.' It could be argued that the resurrection is not significant, because the important aspect of the mission of Christ was to die on the cross so that humanity might be saved. It is Jesus's death, rather than his resurrection, that is the crucial factor. Hooker writes: '...it is the story of how Jesus was glorified and how he glorified God through his death...the story of Christ triumphant on the cross, at one with God.'

e It is important in such questions to stick closely to the point and avoid the temptation simply to tell the story of the crucifixion. The candidate makes it clear from the start exactly what the symbolism of the crucifixion is. There is ample textual evidence and this is used together with extensive references from the Old Testament, supported by relevant examples from the Gospel narrative. Text is used wisely to develop themes and is neatly interwoven with the views of scholars, which are clearly expressed in fluent technical language. In the second part of the answer, a full and proper evaluation is made, highlighting arguments both for and against the significance of the resurrection — something that many candidates fail to do. This is a well-structured A-grade response to a potentially difficult question.

Identify three key features of the crucifixion narrative early on in your studies and use them as the basis for practising essays on this topic. This will help you to avoid storytelling in your answers. Do not neglect the resurrection narrative — chapter 24 is substantial and offers plenty of good material for discussion.

The purpose of the Fourth Gospel

Examine and comment critically on the views of scholars concerning the purpose of the author of the Fourth Gospel.　　　(40 marks)

Why did the Fourth Evangelist write the Gospel? The answer lies, at least in part, in his own words in 20:31: '...these are written that you may believe that Jesus is the Christ, the Son of God, and that by believing you may have life in his name.' However, it seems as though there are two purposes: to bring non-believers to a place of faith for the first time and to encourage those who already believe to continue in their faith. The internal evidence of the text appears to support this. From the very start of the Gospel the author sets out to appeal to all readers. He attracts Jewish readers by his references to the Old Testament scriptures and appeals to Greek readers with the dualistic ideas of light and darkness. Furthermore, he attracts non-believers by promising them 'the right to become children of God' (1:12). Believers are offered the shared experience of God: 'From the fullness of his grace we have all received one blessing after another' (1:16). As Stephen Smalley observes of the author: 'His aim, it appears, is to invite his readers to believe and live.'

Looking at the author's stated purpose in more detail, he reinforces his first claim that 'Jesus is the Christ', by referring to Old Testament prophecies that reveal how Jesus is the One promised by the scriptures. (The word 'Christ' comes from the Greek *Christos*, which means 'Anointed One' and is a Greek translation of the Hebrew word *Messiah*.) Smalley writes: '...on the basis of the evidence marshalled, his readers may have eyes to see that Jesus is the life-giving messiah and Son of God.'

The author links the prophecies of the coming of the Messiah with the actions of Jesus himself. Thus, he cleanses the temple (2:13–17), which was the promised messianic action of Psalm 69:9: 'Zeal for your house will consume me.' Furthermore, his disciples confess who he is (1:41,49) and he reveals this secret to the Samaritan woman (4:25–26). Most significantly, he makes a triumphal entry into Jerusalem riding a donkey in fulfilment of prophecy (12:12–19), reflecting Zechariah 9:9: 'Do not be afraid, O daughter of Zion; see, your king is coming, seated on a donkey's colt.' Finally, the author constantly refers to the refusal of the Jewish authorities to accept him as the Messiah (5:18, 7:47, 10:33, 19:7). As R. V. Tasker notes: 'The supreme wonder of the incarnation was that He who had come down from heaven was revealing Himself not as a demigod, but as the Son of man without in any way ceasing to be divine; and that the climax of that revelation would be when this Son of man, despised, humiliated and rejected would be exalted by being lifted up on a cross.'

The message is reinforced by the miraculous signs, which the author has selected for the purpose of promoting and encouraging belief in Christ, for they demonstrate the reality of Christ as the promised Messiah. Thus, he fed the 5,000 (9:15), as God fed his people with the manna in Exodus, and gave sight to a blind man, to fulfil the prophecy of Isaiah 61:1. Furthermore, the raising of Lazarus from the dead, along with Jesus's declaration — 'I am the resurrection and the life. He who believes in me will live, even though he dies' (11:25) — were meant to encourage and support the persecuted believers facing death in the arenas of Rome and also to impress non-believers with a divine being who could bring life to the dead. As the Jewish authorities themselves said: 'If we let him go on like this, everyone will believe in him' (11:48).

The author's second claim is to prove that Jesus is 'the Son of God', referring to Jesus's divine origin. At the start of the Gospel, John the Baptist testifies that '...this is the Son of God' (1:34), and throughout the Gospel, Jesus refers continually to his intimate relationship with the Father. He knows the Father's will and he and the Father are one (3:35, 5:19–20, 14:10). These claims, which the Jews saw as blasphemous, would lead to his death: 'We have a law, and according to that law he must die, because he claimed to be the Son of God' (19:7).

Finally, the author claims that '...by believing you may have life in his name'. Here the author uses various examples to show that eternal life comes from believing in Christ. John the Baptist calls him 'the Lamb of God, who takes away the sin of the world' (1:29) and in 3:16 we read that '...whoever believes in him shall not perish, but have eternal life'. Later, Jesus speaks of laying down his life for the sheep (10:11) and offers himself as a sacrifice for others (12:24, 17:9). Tasker notes: 'His whole incarnate life is, in fact, meaningless apart from "the hour" to which it is inevitably moving, and that hour is none other than the hour of His passion.'

However, scholars have concluded that the purpose of the author of the Fourth Gospel may be more than these things and there may be other purposes. Clement of Alexandria believed that the Fourth Gospel was written not to convey historically accurate facts but to tell vital spiritual truths about Jesus in order to lead people to believe in him: 'John, perceiving that the external facts had been made plain in the Gospels, being urged by his friends and inspired by the Spirit, composed a spiritual Gospel.'

B. F. Westcott said that the author deliberately altered the historical events in Jesus's life in order to highlight important spiritual truths. Thus, the author places the cleansing of the Temple at the start of Jesus's ministry to make the point that Jesus had come to bring in a new era of spiritual truth based on grace, rather than the law. Similarly, the author alters the timing of Jesus's death, by bringing it forward 24 hours to identify the death of Jesus with the slaughtering of the sacrificial lambs (19:33). Comparing the Fourth Gospel with the other Gospels, Westcott remarked: 'The real difference is that the earliest Gospel contained the fundamental facts and words which experience afterwards interpreted, while the latest Gospel reveals the facts in the light of their interpretation.'

The Gospel may have been written with the additional purpose of correcting the doctrines of Gnosticism and Docetism, which suggested that God could not become flesh and that Jesus was just a special man through whom God revealed himself. The author highlights not only Jesus's divine qualities and origins but also his humanity — thus Jesus weeps (11:35), feels weary (4:6), feels thirsty (19:28) and is raised to life in bodily form. R. V. Tasker supports this view: 'It is on the true humanity of the Saviour that this evangelist throughout his Gospel lays great stress.'

Finally, modern writers suggest other purposes. C. K. Barrett thought that the Gospel was written for a Jewish Church in a Gentile area. Stephen Smalley, in *John: Evangelist and Interpreter*, argued that the Gospel had a message of salvation for all humanity, and J. A. T. Robinson, in *Redating the New Testament*, argued that the Gospel was written to convert Jews to Christianity.

In conclusion, it might be said that the author's purpose was to present the spiritual message of eternal life though Jesus Christ to all believers, and to enable them to bring non-believers into the faith. As Stephen Smalley declared: 'The Christ of St John invites people not only to live, but also to go on living in him.'

This essay achieves an A grade because it offers clear knowledge and understanding of the issues involved, backed up with evidence and scholarship. There is good range of textual referencing, including Old Testament sources that support the material from the Gospel itself. The views of scholars are clearly expressed and themes are developed fluently with comprehensive use of religious language. Key points are examined and commented upon, and arguments are viewed from both sides and backed up with scholarship and textual evidence. The conclusion is thought provoking and shows an understanding that goes beyond the moral response.

You should blend scholarship and textual knowledge in such an essay. Lists of scholars and their views alone are tedious and do not show that you have absorbed much of the biblical text; textual material needs to be put into a scholarly context.

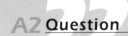

The Prologue to the Fourth Gospel

Examine and consider critically the views of scholars concerning the nature and meaning of the Prologue to the Fourth Gospel. (40 marks)

The Prologue is an enigma — it is one of the most profound, important pieces of theological writing, yet scholars remain unsure about its exact meaning and whether it is an original part of the Gospel or a later addition. J. A. T. Robinson suggests that it is a later addition, probably by another writer, which draws together all the different themes of the Gospel. Burney suggests that it is an Aramaic hymn, written in poetic form with simple construction and frequent use of the word 'and', which was characteristic of such poetry. He argues that it was translated poorly into Greek (e.g. 1:5), indicating that it was of Aramaic origin. C. K. Barrett disagrees, claiming that the Prologue is in a style unique to John, with a thematic approach and with the use of Greek language and syntax that have no Aramaic equivalent (e.g. 1:10). He suggests that it could be a Christological hymn speaking of Christ's heavenly origins.

Whatever the Prologue is, it opens up the Gospel themes to the reader. Stephen Smalley writes: 'The first chapter of John as a whole...appears to be a microcosm of the Fourth Gospel *in toto*.' It enables us to see how the Gospel narrative will unfold and develop — we know how the story starts, develops and ends before we begin to read the Gospel. Not surprisingly, therefore, Stanton calls it a 'lens' through which to view the rest of the Gospel, and Morna Hooker says it is: '...the key that enables us to understand his Gospel'.

Moreover, the Prologue is written for all readers. It contains elements of Jewish and Greek philosophy, which would appeal to the educated peoples of the known world: 'The relation between creation and salvation, prophets and apostles, history and that beyond history, time and eternity, law and grace, death and life, faith and unbelief — these are the themes of the Fourth Gospel' (Hoskyns and Davey). In the Prologue, the author makes it clear that Jesus Christ is God himself, who came into the world as a human being.

The Prologue starts with the Logos — the Word made flesh. Christ's origin is traced back before creation, to '...the beginning'. The author then brings in the overriding themes of the Gospel: light, life, darkness, conflict, witness, sin, new birth, glory and truth. John Marsh suggests that the Logos is 'the satisfying rational principle for understanding the universe'. The Word is the eternal purpose of God and the source of life and creation — the source of light for humanity, which the darkness of the world can never put out: 'Through him all things were made; without him nothing was made that has been made. In him was life and that life was the light of men' (1:3–4).

The author brings from Judaism the idea of God's creative breath (*ruah*), for when God speaks, things happen. According to John Marsh, the author also incorporates the Greek notions of the ideal world and the ideal human. He claimed that the Gospel was '...a meeting place, in a historic person, at a specific moment in human history, of time and eternity, of God and man, of all that lies beyond history and what takes place in it'.

John the Baptist is portrayed by the author as the one sent from God to offer testimony of the coming of the light into the world. Stanton suggests that he is more accurately described as John the Witness because the Word of God is known through his testimony. Rudolf Bultmann suggested that the purpose of the Gospel may be to demonstrate to followers of John that he was not the Messiah and that they should transfer their faith to Jesus. 'He came as a witness to testify to the light, so that through him all men might believe' (1:7).

Bultmann linked this to the Gnostic elements in the Prologue, for example the emphasis on light and dark, which suggests that Christ is the heavenly redeemer who links heaven and earth and brings the wisdom that leads to eternal life and who will ignite the divine spark in all people: 'The true light that gives light to every man was coming into the world' (1:9).

The author makes it clear that Jesus Christ is the incarnate word of God, which has existed from the beginning. This is a gift of God's grace to all who believe and one that establishes a new relationship between God and humanity. This is what some have called the 'scandal' of the Prologue — that the divine word of God can take on human form and live among humanity: 'The Word became flesh and made his dwelling among us' (1:14). Augustine claimed that the notion that the Word could take on flesh was utterly unheard of in Greek philosophy but confirmed what the Old Testament scriptures had declared: 'O that you would rend the heavens and come down...' (Isaiah 64:1).

For Morna Hooker, the real message of the Prologue is that it is concerned with a '...gigantic take-over bid. The old, established firm is Judaism. The newcomers are the Christians, and they lay claim to everything within Judaism. But the basis of their claim is...that the original founder of the firm had intended them to take it over....' Hooker suggested that this message is played out throughout the Gospel: at the wedding in Cana, the cleansing of the Temple, in the conflict with the authorities and on the cross itself. Jesus comes to die and bring salvation: 'The law was given through Moses; grace and truth came through Jesus Christ' (1:17). In doing so, Jesus accomplishes a victory that the Law of Moses could not achieve.

🄴 This essay merits an A grade because it demonstrates clear knowledge and understanding of the issues involved and offers a range of good examples, backed up with textual evidence and scholarship. The candidate clearly understands the context and background to the Prologue and avoids simply listing what is in the Prologue. He/she does not state the obvious and uses scholarly opinion wisely to amplify important points. There is a fluent explanation of the meaning of the various passages, with a good spread of supporting texts, linked to a range of Old Testament material that underpins the Gospel itself. The views of scholars are clearly expressed and themes are developed with impressive use of specialist language. There is critical evaluation of the issues, key points are commented on, and arguments are backed up with scholarship and textual evidence.

There is a danger with such questions that good candidates swamp their answers with scholarly opinions without demonstrating any awareness of the meaning or significance of the text. You need to combine your knowledge of scholarly contributions with textual understanding to ensure that you get a top grade.

Conflict in the Fourth Gospel

Explain the reasons why Jesus came into conflict with the
religious authorities in the Fourth Gospel. Evaluate why the
political authorities sentenced Jesus to death. (40 marks)

The religious authorities did not understand who Jesus was and were afraid of him
because they believed that he posed a threat to Judaism and to the peace of Israel. Jesus
was a challenge to the traditional system of Jewish law, worship and ritual. Crucially,
he claimed to be the Son of God, with a unique relationship with God. They regarded
him as a false prophet, which meant that, under the Law of Moses, he was punishable
by death: 'A prophet who presumes to speak in my name anything I have not
commanded him to say...must be put to death' (Deuteronomy 18:20). In the words
of the Gospel writer, they lived in darkness and would not accept him: 'The light shines
in the darkness, but the darkness has not understood it...he came to that which was
his own, but his own did not receive him' (1:5,11).

This conflict begins early in the ministry of Jesus, when he entered the Temple area and
overturned the stalls of the market traders and money-lenders who were exploiting the
worshippers (2:12–25). By this action, Jesus was making a direct challenge to the
authority of the religious leaders. The prophets Isaiah and Malachi had foretold that the
Messiah would come one day and cleanse the Temple. In Psalm 51:16 God states that
he does not want sacrificial worship and, as John Marsh noted, Jesus, by his actions, was
making clear the fact that salvation comes not from sacrificing animals but from faith
in him.

Jesus challenged the religious leaders by questioning their authority and interpretation
of the law. In chapter 5, Jesus healed a crippled man on the Sabbath. The religious
authorities did not see the healing as an act of God but as a deliberate and punishable
breaking of the law, particularly the requirement to keep the Sabbath day holy (Exodus
20:8). Moreover, Jesus declared that he was the Son of God — a direct challenge to the
status and authority of the Jewish leaders: 'For this reason the Jews tried all the harder
to kill him; not only was he breaking the Sabbath, but he was even calling God his own
father, making himself equal with God' (5:18). Ellis Rivkin observed: 'It was not easy
for the authorities to decide what to do about charismatic leaders who preached no
violence...Were these charismatics harmless preachers, or were they troublemakers?'

The religious authorities refused even to consider that Jesus may be who he claimed
to be. In their 'darkness', they questioned Jesus's origins (8:19), and accused him of false
prophecy and sorcery (7:12,47). For the author of the Gospel, the religious authorities
belong to the world that cannot recognise and rejects Jesus: 'If God were your father,
you would love me, for I came from God...You belong to your father, the devil'

(8:42–44). Jesus healed a blind man and declared himself to be the 'light of the world' (8:12). The authorities, in their darkness, accused Jesus of lying and questioned the legitimacy of his relationship with God. They did not understand who he was, as Alan Culpepper observed, in *The Anatomy of the Fourth Gospel*: 'By not having heard or seen the father, they are Jesus's opposite; in their response to Jesus they are the opposite of the disciples.' Jesus condemned the religious authorities for not being prepared to see, hear or believe in him: 'You are from below; I am from above. You are of this world; I am not of this world...The reason you do not hear is that you do not belong to God' (8:23,47).

The authorities responded by repeating their accusation that Jesus is a sinner because he broke the Sabbath laws by healing the man. They used the law, which, according to Psalm 119:105, was their light, in order to keep themselves in the darkness: 'If you were blind, you would not be guilty of sin; but now that you claim you can see, your guilt remains' (9:41). Later, Jesus spoke of himself as the 'gate for the sheep' (10:7) and the 'good shepherd' (10:11), reflecting the Old Testament image of a shepherd as a guardian of the people and also as their king (Ezekiel 34). Jesus likened the religious authorities to the 'hired hand' (10:12) who do not care for the sheep. Jesus is the good shepherd who will 'lay down my life for the sheep' (10:15). The authorities are not the real and trusted leaders of God's people. Inevitably, the religious leaders became enraged, and when Jesus declared that 'I and the Father are one' (10:30), they accused him of blasphemy and tried to stone him.

The fear that the religious authorities have of Jesus is most starkly shown after the raising of Lazarus. By now the crowds believed in Jesus, which threatened the authority and power of the religious leaders. This prompted Caiaphas, the High Priest, to declare a radical solution to the issue: '...it is better for you that one man die for the people than that the whole nation perish' (11:50). Shortly after this, Jesus entered Jerusalem, fulfilling Zechariah's prophecy that the king of Israel would enter in such a way. This blatant attack on the authority of the religious leaders led to Jesus's arrest, trial and eventual crucifixion — with the Jews trapped in their own darkness. John Marsh observes: '...good men are driven to evil sometimes by the very soundness of their good intentions.'

The Romans were the political authority. They wanted to collect taxes and to keep the nation in a state of peace. Thus the Romans required the religious authorities to deal firmly with any potential troublemakers. Only the Romans, as the political authority, could pass the death sentence, or *ius gladii*. So the religious authorities brought Jesus before Pilate. Blasphemy was not a crime in Roman law, so the Jews accused Jesus simply of being 'a criminal' (18:30).

Pilate was uncomfortable with the whole matter. He declared that he found no basis for a charge against Jesus. However, Pilate knew that he should not anger the religious authorities, because he depended on them to keep the peace. As a way out, he asked the people to choose, but the crowd shouted for Pilate to release a prisoner called

Barabbas. Stephen Smalley notes: 'The contrast between Jesus and his enemies — who are also the enemies of God — as darkness, is sustained throughout the Gospel, particularly in the debates between Jesus and the Jews.'

Pilate condemned Jesus to death because he was afraid, not of Jesus, but of what the religious authorities might do. He was being used as a pawn in a power game between Jesus and the religious authorities. The author of the Gospel makes it clear that he believes that it was the religious and not the political authorities who were responsible for the death of Jesus — not acting not out of malice or evil, but out of fear and a misunderstanding of who Jesus was. According to Alan Culpepper: 'Although they do not recognise who Jesus is, there is wilfulness in their blindness. They love darkness rather than light.'

e The positive introduction sets the scene and the candidate identifies the key issues and characters, using religious terms and textual context and background. In answering such a question it is crucial to refer to the law in Deuteronomy, but most candidates fail to mention it. There is excellent use of the Old Testament background material — the meaning and interpretation of these words lie at the heart of the conflict. The candidate addresses the issues clearly and directly, using scholarly sources supported by textual evidence. There is also useful evaluation of complex issues, motives and arguments and good use of religious language. There is a well-informed and clear analysis of the issues, and a very detailed coverage of the fears of the religious authorities, supported by textual evidence and the views of scholars. The candidate offers a modern alternative to traditional viewpoints. The final quotation is direct, powerful and challenging — an excellent way to end a thought-provoking essay.

e **Do not rely on a narrative approach, based on endless retelling of Jesus's conflicts with the Pharisees, especially the Sabbath controversies. The key issue is deeper, as demonstrated by the high level of scholarship in this answer.**

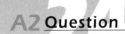
The crucifixion and resurrection in the Fourth Gospel

Examine the religious symbolism contained in the account of the crucifixion in the Fourth Gospel. To what extent was the resurrection an important aspect of Jesus's ministry? (40 marks)

The account of the crucifixion in the Fourth Gospel is surprisingly brief, but the author uses much symbolism from the Old Testament to convey the most important aspect of his message, namely that everything is done under God's own control — through Christ's actions, the scriptures are fulfilled and salvation is at hand. As Raymond Brown observed, Jesus is 'the sole master of his destiny'.

The Old Testament symbolism is evident throughout. It begins with Jesus carrying his own cross, just as Isaac carried the wood upon which he was to be sacrificed (Genesis 22:6). Jesus is crucified between 'two others' (19:18), whom we think are criminals, though the author does not specify so. Indeed, they appear to be the 'transgressors' prophesied in Isaiah 53:12. In addition, Jesus himself seemed to predict crucifixion as his form of execution: 'But I, when I am lifted up from the earth, will draw all men to myself' (12:32). He knows, too, that such a death brings condemnation: '...anyone who is hung on a tree is under God's curse' (Deuteronomy 21:23). More fulfilment of the scriptures follows. Jesus's clothes were divided by lot among the soldiers, as suggested in Psalm 22:18: 'They divided my clothes among them and cast lots for my clothing.' Moreover, Jesus is wearing a seamless robe, which is suggestive of the sacred garment known as the ephod, which was worn by the High Priest — God's representative on Earth (Exodus 28:31).

Jesus's mother is there and he gives her to the care of the disciple whom he loved (19:25–27). His mother was there at the start of his ministry during the wedding at Cana and is present at the end to witness its fulfilment and climax. Joseph Grassi observes: 'Jesus's last will established the blessed disciple as his successor and son by having his own mother continue the relationship by adopting the blessed disciple as her own son.'

On the cross Jesus says 'I am thirsty' (19:28) and the soldiers give him vinegar to drink, fulfilling the words of Psalm 69:21: 'They put gall in my food and gave me vinegar for my thirst.' As Jesus comes close to death, there are several symbolic references to the Passover. He is given vinegar to drink from a sponge on the top of a hyssop plant

(19:29). In the story of the Passover, the Israelites were saved from death when the blood of the lamb was painted on to their doorframes from a hyssop plant (Exodus 12:22). In keeping with the imagery of the Passover lamb, Jesus dies without the need for having his legs broken, just as the bones of the Passover sacrificial lamb are not broken: '...he protects all his bones, not one of them will be broken' (Psalm 34:20).

Jesus even has control over the time of his death. He bows his head, causing John Marsh to observe that he 'deliberately chose his moment of death by bowing his head, thus restricting his breathing and causing life to become extinct'. In addition, the author of the Gospel places Jesus's crucifixion at the same time as the priests would be slaughtering the Passover lambs (between noon and nightfall). This reinforces the view, first put forward by John the Baptist, that Jesus is the 'lamb of God' (1:29). In *John as Storyteller*, Mark Stibbe wrote: 'The idea of the death of Christ as a paschal sacrifice is therefore one theme in this final act of John's passion narrative.'

Finally, Jesus's side is pierced by a spear, as prophesied in Zechariah 12:10: 'They will look on me, the one they have pierced' and in Isaiah 53:5: '...he was pierced for our transgressions'. Blood and water flow from his side — symbolic of the blood of salvation and the water of baptism and new life, fulfilling the words of Psalm 22:14,16: 'I am poured out like water...a band of evil men has encircled me, they have pierced my hands and my feet.'

The notion of water and blood as a means of spiritual renewal was well known in Judaism. In Leviticus 14:1ff, the Law of Moses speaks of the ritual cleansing of lepers by means of blood and water. So the blood and water from Jesus's side represent a spiritual cleansing. This is particularly significant. Earlier in his mission, at the wedding at Cana (2:1–11) Jesus replaced the inadequate water of Jewish purification with the rich wine of the Gospel, later to be symbolised by his blood. Later, he told Nicodemus of the need to be reborn in water and Spirit. Similarly, he spoke to the Samaritan woman of the 'living water' (4:10), which in 7:39 is crucial for salvation: 'Whoever believes in me, as the Scripture has said, streams of living water will flow from within him' (7:38).

Even the burial of Christ has symbolic elements. Joseph of Arimathea and Nicodemus take him to a new tomb, reminiscent of Isaiah's prophecy of the suffering servant being 'with the rich in his death' (53:9). They wrap the body in myrrh and linen cloths (Psalm 45:8) and bury Jesus before the beginning of the Sabbath, as required by the Law (Deuteronomy 21:23).

The resurrection is important because it reveals significant spiritual truths. First, it is the final sign, showing the completion of God's saving work. The empty tomb is the proof of the reality of the resurrection and confirms Jesus's teaching: '...unless a grain of wheat falls to the ground and dies, it remains only a single seed. But if it dies, it produces many seeds' (12:24).

Second, the resurrection is the fulfilment of scripture and enables the disciples to go out into the world and preach the Gospel: '...you will not abandon me to the grave, nor will you let your Holy One see decay' (Psalm 16:10). Jesus is buried in a tomb in a garden — just as the Garden of Eden was the place where life began, so in this garden will life be renewed. As R. V. Tasker observed: '...the fall of the first Adam took place in a garden; and it was in a garden that the second Adam redeemed mankind.' The author highlights this by reference to Mary Magdalene, who first gave the news of the resurrection. As Robert Kysar noted: 'She is cast in the eminent role as the first to discover the empty tomb, the first to witness the risen Christ, and the first to announce the good news of the resurrection. Not even Peter or the beloved disciple is so privileged.'

Third, the resurrection breaks down the barrier between God and humanity: 'And if I go and prepare a place for you, I will come back and take you to be with me...I am the way and the truth and the life. No one comes to the father except through me' (14:3,6).

The author uses Thomas's doubt to demonstrate to all future believers that Christ has risen and that they can believe without the benefit of physical proof: '...blessed are those who have not seen and yet have believed' (20:29). Alan Culpepper suggests: 'Thomas is the opposite of Peter, who saw Jesus's glory but could not accept his suffering...Thomas stands in for all those who...embrace the earthly Jesus but have yet to recognise the risen Christ.'

Finally, and most importantly, the resurrection represents the culmination of God's provision of atonement and salvation and is the dawning of a new age. As Stephen Smalley observes: 'This is the heart of the matter...in the whole of the Fourth Gospel; the new age of fulfilment is here, and Judaism has been replaced by Christianity.'

e This is a popular question, but it not always well answered. It is important to stick closely to the requirements of the question and avoid the temptation simply to tell the story of the crucifixion. This candidate makes it clear from the start exactly what the symbolism of the crucifixion is. There is ample textual evidence, which is used together with extensive references from the Old Testament. This is the heart of the answer: Old Testament symbolism, supported by relevant examples from the Gospel narrative. Text is used wisely to develop themes and is neatly interwoven with the views of scholars. This is a well-structured and thoughtful response to a potentially difficult question.

e **Identify three key features of the crucifixion narrative early on in your studies and use them as the basis for practising essays on this topic. This will help you to avoid simple storytelling. Do not neglect the resurrection narrative — chapters 20 and 21 are substantial and offer plenty of good material for discussion.**